ROCKS ABOVE THE CLOUDS

THE COLORADO MOUNTAIN CLUB PACK GUIDE

ROCKS ABOVE THE CLOUDS

A Hiker's and Climber's Guide to Colorado Mountain Geology

Jack Reed and Gene Ellis

U.S. Geological Survey

The Colorado Mountain Club Press

PUBLISHED BY:

The Colorado Mountain Club Press
710 Tenth Street, #200, Golden, Colorado 80401
303-279-3080 ext. 2 | email: cmcpress@cmc.org

Founded in 1912, The Colorado Mountain Club is the largest outdoor recreation, education, and conservation organization in the Rocky Mountains. Look for our books at your local bookstore or outdoor retailer or online at www.cmc.org

DISTRIBUTED TO THE BOOK TRADE BY:

Mountaineers Books
1001 SW Klickitat Way, Suite 201, Seattle, WA 98134, 800-553-4453
www.mountaineersbooks.org

COVER IMAGE: Linda Reed on the summit of Crestone. Photo by Jack Reed.
INTERIOR IMAGES: All images by the authors, except as credited on individual photographs.

Alan Bernhard—design and composition
Alex Goulder—copyeditor
Christine Silvestri—proofreader
Alan Stark—publisher

We gratefully acknowledge the financial support of the people of Colorado through the Scientific and Cultural Facilities District of greater metropolitan Denver for our publishing activities.

ISBN 978-0-9760525-8-6

Printed in China

DEDICATION

This book is dedicated to
Ogden L. Tweto (1912–1983),
who was a U.S. Geological Survey geologist
for more than forty years
and the author of the
Geologic Map of Colorado (USGS 1979).
He spent his career studying the
geology of the mountains he loved,
and his work has guided
all who follow in his footsteps.
His memory was honored
by the naming of Mount Tweto (13,619 ft.)
in the Mosquito Range near Climax.

Contents

Acknowledgments

We GRATEFULLY ACKNOWLEDGE our many colleagues at the U.S. Geological Survey who have generously shared their knowledge of Colorado geology and provided invaluable guidance in the preparation of this book. We are especially indebted to Jeremy Havens who assisted with the preparation of the maps and drawings and offered advice on the intricacies of computer graphics programs. He and Cal Ruleman acted as technical reviewers of the manuscript, and their thoughtful suggestions helped clarify some of our rather muddy writing efforts. Paco Van Sistine helped with the satellite imagery and the preparation of the shaded-relief models.

We also acknowledge the generosity of our U.S.G.S. colleagues, The Colorado Mountain Club members, and many others who magnanimously allowed us to use their photographs. These include James Aber, Russ Allen, Harlan Barton, Bruce Bryant, Tom Chapel, Dave Gaskill, Stewart Green, Steve Hoffmeyer, Bernie Hohman, Karl Kellogg, Ulli Limpitlaw, Kay Miller, George Moore, Ken Nolan, Bob Pearson, Doug Richards, and Van Williams. Their pictures are identified in the captions. We also thank those who submitted pictures for consideration, but whose pictures were not selected. We are indebted to Gary Landeck of The American Alpine Club Library for helping us locate the picture from The Colorado Mountain Club archives, and to the Grand Teton Natural History Association for allowing us to reuse the glacier diagram that originally appeared in one of their publications.

Preparation of the book was partly funded by the Bradley Scholarship Program of the U.S. Geological Survey.

Preface

Thinking Like a Geologist

"And some run up hill and down dale,
knapping the chucky stanes to pieces wi' hammers
like sae many road-makers gone daft.
They say 'tis to see how the world was made."

SIR WALTER SCOTT
1825

What do geologists see when they wander through the mountains? Can they read the rocks and immediately understand the building of continents, the slow grinding down of rocks, and the inexorable progression of evolution?

If only it were that easy. Scientific knowledge might produce some answers, but it also results in additional questions. And that is the way it should be. Life and the wonderful world around us would be too simple and mundane if a little book learning and a few years of experience enabled us to comprehend fully the magnificent diversity of our environment. Gaining knowledge of the geology will help you understand some of what you find in the mountain environment, but it will also make you aware that there is always another mystery lurking around the next ridge or beyond the pass.

We invite you to keep an open mind as you trudge up that seemingly endless slope of loose blocks. Did these blocks fall from the cliff directly above, or were they deposited by a retreating glacier during the Pleistocene Ice Age? When you curse the knee-deep mire in the valley bottom, are you wallowing in muck that backed up behind a landslide? When the ground changes from firm, well-drained sand and gravel to loose, slippery clay, have you crossed over from soil underlain by sandstone to soil underlain by shale? These are just a few of the questions that a geologically inclined adventurer might ask.

Sometimes a little knowledge of geology can ease your way and maybe even help you avoid an awkward or dangerous situation. Knowing something about different rock types might enable you to pick a route that avoids loose rock. Knowing that a particular rock surface will feel like grease with just a little water might encourage you to forego that siesta on the summit and head down before the afternoon thunderstorm.

Keep your eyes and your mind open in the mountains. Doing so will increase your enjoyment as well as enhance your chances of survival. We promise you will notice things you once took for granted.

Introduction

"And yet these Mountains we are speaking of, to confess the truth, are nothing but great ruines; but such as show a certain magnificence in Nature. . . ."

THOMAS BRUNET
from "*The Sacred Theory of the Earth*", 1681–1689

Mountains might be perceived as nothing but inanimate piles of rocks. Yet almost anyone who frequents the Colorado mountains would agree that different ranges and even different peaks seem to have distinct personalities and auras. Contrast the stable white slabs and faces of Mount Eolus or Sunlight Peak with the treacherous unstable ledges of the Maroon Bells, or the somber gray cliffs and talus slopes of Grays and Torreys Peaks with the jagged ridges and faces of the Crestones. Consider the differences between the irregular varicolored ramparts of the western San Juans and the soaring gray pinnacles of the Needle Mountains.

All of these differences are rooted in the rocks that compose them and in the processes of uplift and erosion that have shaped them. In short, it all goes back to geology. Whether you travel in the mountains as a casual hiker, a peak bagger, or a technical climber, a knowledge of mountain geology can help in planning your route, selecting your campsites, and evaluating the hazards you may face; but perhaps most importantly, it can enhance your understanding and appreciation of the wonders of the mountain landscape.

What makes a mountain? The surface of the Earth is a battleground between forces that uplift parts of the Earth's crust and the processes of erosion that are constantly at work attempting to level the uplifts and reduce the landscape to a near-level plain. Mountains form wherever the rate of uplift exceeds the rate of erosion for a significant span of geologic time. The forces of uplift include movement of tectonic plates, eruption of lava and volcanic debris to form volcanoes, and slow upwelling of hot viscous material from the Earth's mantle (the layer that lies beneath the crust). The processes of erosion include movement of surface material by wind, flash floods, rockfalls, landslides, avalanches, and slow down-slope creep of soil and rocks due to freezing and thawing. In high mountains such as the Colorado Rockies, the work of glaciers has been especially important in shaping the landscape.

What is a "Fourteener"?

Colorado peaks with summits higher than 14,000 feet are commonly referred to as "Fourteeners". But how many of them are there? Various guidebooks give various numbers, depending on how each particular author chooses to define a separate peak. In 1968, in an article in *Trail & Timberline* (the magazine of The Colorado Mountain Club), William Graves suggested that to be considered a separate Fourteener a peak should be separated from a neighboring Fourteener by a saddle that is at least 300 feet lower than the summit of the lower peak. This rule has been widely accepted and has been generally honored by The Colorado Mountain Club in its various publications. When the rule was proposed, modern topographic surveys had not yet been completed. When the surveys were finished in the 1970s, it was discovered that North Maroon Peak and El Diente, both of which had traditionally been considered separate peaks, failed to meet the 300-foot criterion. However, out of respect for tradition, they continued to be included in most Fourteener lists, bringing the total number of Fourteeners to 54. This is the number that is most widely quoted and is the one we have used in this book. However, the 10th edition of *Guide to the Colorado Mountains* published by The Colorado Mountain Club in 2000 drops North Maroon and El Diente from the list and adds Challenger Point (near Kit Carson Mountain), making a total of 53 Fourteeners. Does it really matter how many Fourteeners there are? Not really, except to peak baggers and hair splitters. As Lou Dawson wrote in his 1999 guidebook "*Rocky Mountain peaks around 14,000 feet in height stand out from other Colorado peaks. They have the greatest vertical drops, summits that leap to the sky, and an imposing majesty that pleases the eye and lifts the spirit.*"

The character of the mountains formed as a result of this ceaseless contest between uplift and erosion depends on many things, including the types of rocks being uplifted, the erosional processes that carve them, and the balance between the rates of uplift and erosion at various times in their history. Uplift of hard, erosion-resistant rock can produce major mountains even if the rate of uplift is slow. Conversely, if the uplifted rocks are soft and easily eroded, very rapid uplift is required to produce mountains. Uplift that involves a wide array of rocks generally produces the most diverse and interesting mountain landscapes. This is certainly true of the Colorado mountains, where a long and complex geologic history has resulted in juxtaposition of many different ages and types of rocks in the blocks of the Earth's crust that were raised and sculpted to form the present mountains.

While the type of rock is critical in determining the general character of a range or peak, many other factors are also involved. Rocks are rarely homogeneous. They are broken by fractures and faults, roughened by weathering, smoothed by glaciers, and variously adorned with moss and lichens. All of these attributes are of concern to the serious climber or mountain traveler. As the famous mountaineer J. H. B. Bell once remarked: *"Any fool can climb good rock, but it takes craft and cunning to get up vegetatious schist and granite."*

Planar fractures in rocks along which no significant movement has occurred are called joints. They are present in almost all natural rock exposures. They have various orientations ranging from vertical to horizontal and commonly occur in sub-parallel (almost parallel) sets with more or less uniform spacing ranging from a few inches to tens or hundreds of feet. Many outcrops display several sets of joints that cause the rock to break into more or less uniform blocks. The orientation and spacing of joints play a major role in determining the character of the cracks, chimneys, and ledges on a rock face, as well as the size, shape, and general stability of the talus at its base. Joints form either as the result of stresses on the rock deep within the Earth's crust or release of pressure and expansion as erosion removes the overlying material to expose it at the surface. Some joints also form as igneous rocks contract while cooling and solidifying at or near the surface.

Faults are fractures or planar zones along which the rocks on one side have moved up, down, or sideways with respect to rocks on the other side. Offsets across faults range from a few inches to several miles, but most faults depicted on geologic maps have offsets of at least several hundred feet. Faults are rarely discrete (simple, undeformed) surfaces. Generally, they are marked by zones of broken and crushed rock a few inches to a few feet thick. Because the shattered rocks are less resistant to erosion, faults are seldom exposed at the surface. However, in the Colorado mountains they are often marked by narrow scree-filled couloirs along which the rocks are stained brown, red, or yellow by oxidation of ore minerals carried by solutions that have percolated along them. Because of the unstable scree and the shattered loose rock along them, fault zones are generally climbing routes of last resort, regardless of the type of rock in which they occur.

Joints in granite.

Rocks exposed at the surface are subject to weathering, both by chemical decomposition of mineral grains and by mechanical breakup. Chemical weathering is caused by exposure to rain and meltwater charged with chemicals picked up from the atmosphere or from vegetation. Chemical weathering is generally slow in mountain environments, but over long periods of time it tends to roughen the surfaces of exposed rocks by removing less resistant mineral grains and leaving more resistant grains projecting

Steeply inclined fault in basement rocks. The zone of crushed and stained rocks along the fault is about six feet wide. In this outcrop it is impossible to tell the direction of relative motion of the rocks on opposite sides of the fault.

from the surface like sandpaper. Mechanical breakup is facilitated by freezing and thawing of water that trickles along fractures, abrasion by windblown sand and snow, wedging by roots, and down-slope creep. Ultimately, more resistant parts of the rock weather out to form bumps or knobs, while less resistant parts form depressions or pockets.

Glaciers smooth and polish rock surfaces over which they flow, chiefly through the process of abrasion by sand and rocks entrained in the moving ice. As recently as 12,000 years ago, all of the major Colorado Ranges were festooned with glaciers and all of the higher valleys filled with ice to depths of hundreds or thousands of feet. Only the summits and highest ridges and uplands escaped the work of the ice. Where the rocks stood above the ice, they have retained the rough surfaces and abundant holds

Thrust fault in sedimentary rocks. The fault (marked by a dashed yellow line) cuts across the bedding in the right side of the photo, but becomes parallel to the beds in the left part of the photo. Direction of movement of the rocks above the fault with respect to those below is shown by the arrow.

formed by weathering before and between the various ice ages; where they lay beneath the ice, the same rocks are rounded and burnished and therefore present entirely different problems to climbers. A similar effect is evident in climbing areas along canyons where rock faces below flood level are polished smooth, while those higher up are weathered and broken and present a wider variety of handholds and footholds.

Although many rock faces in the high mountains are bare of vegetation, most are embellished to some degree with mosses, lichens, and other slippery plants. While these add to the beauty of the alpine scene, they can also increase the difficulty of the climb. A damp rock face covered with moss or coated with lichen is a problem, no matter what kind of rock it is! The extent and the character of these plants depends on such factors as amount of moisture, exposure to light and wind, time of snow melt, and the type of rock on which they grow.

ONE

The Rocks of the Mountains

What the Colorado Mountains Are Made Of

"...The surface of the ground, so dull and forbidding at first sight, besides being rich in plants, shines and sparkles with crystals: mica, hornblende, feldspar, quartz, tourmaline. The radiance in some places is so great as to be fairly dazzling, keen lance rays of every color sparkling in glorious abundance, joining the plants in their fine brave beauty-work—every crystal, every flower a window opening into heaven...."

JOHN MUIR

from *"My first summer in the Sierra"*, 1911

Mountains are made of rocks, but what is a rock? A rock is any naturally occurring coherent aggregate of mineral grains. But what is a mineral? A mineral is a naturally occurring inorganic element or compound having a characteristic chemical composition, crystal form, and physical properties. There are hundreds, if not thousands, of known minerals, but only a relative handful make up the vast majority of the rocks that we see in traveling the Colorado mountains. Exhibit 1 lists some of the most common.

EXHIBIT 1

Common Rock-forming Minerals

(Listed in order of abundance in Colorado rocks.)

NAME: Quartz
COMPOSITION: SiO_2 silicon dioxide
CHARACTERISTICS: Gray, white, or clear; hard with glassy luster. Breaks in irregular fragments. Very resistant to chemical decay. Sometimes forms clear six-sided crystals.
WHERE FOUND: A major constituent of most mountain rocks.

NAME: Potassium feldspar
COMPOSITION: $KAlSi_3O_8$ potassium-aluminum silicate
CHARACTERISTICS: Pink, gray, or white, with pearly luster. Not quite as hard as quartz, breaks easily into tabular shiny pieces. Commonly shows tartan-like pattern on broken faces.
WHERE FOUND: Common in granite and related rocks; also widespread in metamorphic rocks and some sedimentary rocks.

NAME: Plagioclase feldspar
COMPOSITION: $(Na,Ca)AlSi_3O_8$ sodium-calcium aluminum silicate
CHARACTERISTICS: Gray or white, with pearly luster. Not quite as hard as quartz, breaks easily into tabular shiny pieces. Commonly shows a pattern of closely spaced parallel lines on broken faces.
WHERE FOUND: Common in granite and related rocks, basalt, and in many metamorphic rocks. Seldom found in sedimentary rocks.

NAME: Biotite (black mica)
COMPOSITION: $K(MgFe)_3AlSi_3O_{10}(OH)_2$
hydrous potassium aluminum silicate with iron and magnesium
CHARACTERISTICS: Black or dark brown, in flakes or tabular crystals. Easily scratched or split into paper thin sheets with a knife.
WHERE FOUND: Common in granite and related rocks, light-colored volcanic rocks, and in many metamorphic rocks. Seldom found in sedimentary rocks.

NAME: **Muscovite** (white mica)
COMPOSITION: $KAl_2AlSi_3O_{10}(OH)_2$
hydrous potassium aluminum silicate
CHARACTERISTICS: Silvery white, in flakes or tabular crystals. Easily scratched or split into paper-thin sheets with a knife.
WHERE FOUND: Common in granite and related rocks, and in metamorphic rocks, especially schist. Seldom found in sedimentary rocks.

NAME: **Hornblende**
COMPOSITION: $Ca_2Na(MgFeAl)_5\ [(SiAl)_4O_{11}]_2(OH)_2$
complex calcium aluminum silicate with sodium, iron, and magnesium
CHARACTERISTICS: Very dark green, in prismatic six-sided crystals. Breaks into prismatic fragments along intersecting planes about 120° apart.
WHERE FOUND: Common in many igneous and metamorphic rocks. Seldom found in sedimentary rocks.

NAME: **Pyroxene**
COMPOSITION: $(CaMgFe)Si_2O_6$
complex calcium magnesium iron silicate
CHARACTERISTICS: Very dark green in stubby prismatic or tabular crystals. Breaks into rectangular fragments along intersecting planes 90° apart.
WHERE FOUND: Common in dark igneous rocks like gabbro and basalt. Seldom found in sedimentary rocks.

NAME: **Clay minerals**
COMPOSITION: A group of hydrous aluminum silicate minerals with various amount of sodium, potassium, iron, and magnesium
CHARACTERISTICS: Gray, white, orange, red, yellow or brown. Individual grains not distinguishable except with electron microscope. Forms soft, putty-like aggregates.
WHERE FOUND: Common in sedimentary rocks, especially shale. Formed in igneous and metamorphic rocks by weathering or by alteration of the original minerals by hot solutions moving along faults and fractures.

NAME: Calcite and dolomite
COMPOSITION: $CaCO_3$ (calcite) and $CaMg(CO_3)_2$ (dolomite)
CHARACTERISTICS: Gray, white, or various other colors. Easily scratched with knife. Break easily in six-sided pieces resembling distorted cubes.
WHERE FOUND: Form sedimentary rocks (limestone and dolomite). Also occur as veins and pockets in igneous and metamorphic rocks.

There are many ways of classifying and describing rocks. For example, a stone mason is most interested in whether a rock breaks in thin slabs, rectangular blocks, or rough, irregular shapes. An architect or interior designer is concerned with the color of the rock and whether it can be cut into slabs and polished to reveal interesting textures and designs. An engineer might focus on the strength of the rock, whether or not it is broken by faults or joints, and how difficult it is to excavate. A mountain hiker probably is interested in whether it should be classified as "talus", "damned talus", or "goddamned talus"!

Geologists are most concerned with how rocks were formed and what they can tell us about geologic history. Accordingly, they classify rocks into three basic groups based on their origins: sedimentary rocks, metamorphic rocks, and igneous rocks. Nothing in nature is ever simple, and rocks are no exception, but these simple categories are a good place to start. Geologists love to name things, and there are thousands of names proposed for various rocks, many of them redundant, and most of them confusing. However, for the purposes of mountain travelers and climbers, it is only necessary to describe the few that are most conspicuous in the Colorado mountains.

SEDIMENTARY ROCKS

Sedimentary rocks are formed by the consolidation of material that has accumulated in layers on the Earth's surface, either on land, in lakes, or on the sea bottom. Many sedimentary rocks are composed of mineral grains or rock fragments derived from decay and erosion of older rocks. Others are composed of minerals that have chemically precipitated from water, generally in lakes, the ocean, or hot springs. A third type of sedimentary rock is composed largely

Talus everywhere—a world of grief! Notice that the talus in the foreground is covered with lichens and is probably relatively stable, while that on the steeper slopes in the background lacks lichen, appears lighter colored, and is probably less stabilized. Walking on it is likely to be rather difficult! ULLI LIMPITLAW PHOTO

of remains or secretions of plants or animals—coal is a good example.

The sedimentary layers, called beds, are a distinctive feature of sedimentary rocks, and their thickness, inclination, and orientation play a major role in shaping the topography of mountains carved from them. The orientation and inclination of the beds strongly influence the problems and possibilities they present to the mountain traveler. If the beds are gently inclined, the mountain slopes very commonly have a stair-step appearance. The beds most resistant to erosion form bands of cliffs, while the softer layers form gentler talus-covered slopes between. Moderately sloping beds present different problems on different sides of the mountain. Where the beds slope into the side of the mountain, the ledges formed by the resistant beds lean inward, the holds formed by the projecting bedding planes are more secure, and the falling rocks are more likely to be caught and stopped behind the inward-sloping ledges. In contrast, where the beds slope away from the mountain side, the ledges and holds tend to slope out, and the danger of rockfall is increased. Where bedding is steep or vertical, resistant layers project as ridges, fins, or flatirons, whereas softer layers erode to form valleys, clefts, and couloirs.

Conglomerate, sandstone, and shale are the most widespread sedimentary rocks in the Colorado mountains. They make up many of the highest and most spectacular peaks and present some of the most challenging climbing, both in the mountains and in technical climbing areas in the foothills. All of these rocks are clastic sedimentary rocks; that is, they are composed of mineral grains and fragments derived from weathering and erosion of older rocks, transported and deposited by water or wind, and

Climbing on gently inclined inward-sloping beds. 1928 Colorado Mountain Club outing on the Maroon Bells. CMC ARCHIVES

later cemented together to form rocks. The cementation of the sediment grains to form sedimentary rocks is partly due to deposition of quartz, calcite, or other minerals from percolating water during and after deposition of the sediment and partly due to compaction by the weight of overlying layers. Conglomerate is formed by cementation of gravel, sandstone by cementation of sand, and shale from clay. The size of the grains and fragments is a clue to how far the sediments have been transported. Gravel is generally deposited close to its source, sand is car-

Climbing up a couloir in steeply inclined beds on Crestone Peak.
TOM CHAPEL PHOTO

ried much farther, and clay is distributed most widely of all. Although all of these clastic rocks have similar origins and commonly occur interleaved or inter-fingered with one another, they differ in appearance, resistance to erosion, and "climbability", and therefore deserve separate descriptions.

CONGLOMERATE: The distinguishing feature of conglomerate is that it contains abundant rounded pieces of older rocks. Rounded pieces between the size of a BB and the size of a baseball are called pebbles, those between a baseball and a soccer ball are cobbles, and those larger than a soccer ball are boulders. Collectively, they are called clasts. Large rounded clasts are evidence of deposition in fast-flowing water, generally close to the source of the gravel. In some conglomerates the clasts are nearly all derived from the same rock. In others, clasts

Conglomerate containing pebbles, cobbles, and boulders of a variety of older rocks cemented in a matrix of sandstone. This rock is part of the wreckage of the Ancestral Rocky Mountains.

represent a wide variety of rocks of different ages and origins. The finer material between the clasts, typically sand or silt, is called the matrix. The color of the rock depends on the colors of both the matrix and the clasts. Typically it is white, gray, or red, but some conglomerates contain clasts with a wide variety of colors.

Conglomerate commonly forms discrete beds interlayered with sandstone, but in some places it forms pods and layers tens or hundreds of feet thick. Well-cemented conglomerate is typically very resistant to erosion and thus tends to form cliffs or ledges among less resistant layers of sandstone and shale. If the clasts are more resistant to weathering and erosion than the matrix, they commonly project on weathered faces, forming magnificent handholds and footholds. If the clasts are less resistant, they weather out to form

Coarse-grained red sandstone, containing scattered quartz pebbles. This sandstone contains abundant feldspar. Red color is due to iron oxide stain on the quartz and feldspar grains. This rock is typical of the "redbeds" formed from debris shed from the Ancestral Rocky Mountains.

hollows and crannies. However, if the conglomerate is not well-cemented, the projecting clasts may pull loose from the matrix with extremely unpleasant results for the incautious climber. Conglomerate tends to break into large, rudely rectangular blocks that form rather stable talus.

SANDSTONE: Sandstone is probably the most abundant sedimentary rock in the higher parts of the Colorado mountains. Sand is composed of rounded mineral grains ranging in size from the size of grains of table salt to the size of BBs. The mineral grains are derived from decay of older rocks and are sorted and rounded as they are transported by wind or water. As a result, the sandstone is formed of minerals that are most resistant to chemical decomposition and to mechanical breakdown. Most sands are composed chiefly of quartz, although some contain appreciable amounts of feldspar and minor amounts of other resistant minerals. When the sand is cemented to form sandstone the individual sand grains are generally easily visible to the naked eye or with a low-power magnifying glass. Sandstones have a wide range of colors including white, gray, yellow, orange, brown, and red, depending largely on the color of the mineral cement.

Sandstone forms uniform beds hundreds of feet thick in the Colorado Plateau, but in the mountains of Colorado it more commonly forms beds a few feet to a few dozen feet thick. Most sandstone is relatively resistant to erosion, so it commonly forms cliff bands, hogbacks, and flatirons, as well as a cap rock on buttes and mesas. It commonly breaks into flat slabs or blocks which are bounded on one face by the surfaces of the beds and on the other faces by joints that are approximately perpendicular to the beds. Where these blocks are small, they form loose and unstable talus. Poorly cemented sandstone tends to weather into rounded shapes and to crumble unpredictably, making it unattractive for scrambling or serious climbing. However, well-cemented sandstone commonly has myriad joints, jam-cracks, and chimneys, as well as good

Fine-grained white sandstone with thin beds of black shale. This sandstone is composed chiefly of quartz grains cemented by clay minerals. It is typical of the sandstone deposited along the shores of the Great Cretaceous Seaway.

friction on the bedding surfaces. Weathering of sandstone commonly produces spectacular knobs, fins, and gargoyles where the more resistant parts of the rock have been etched out by blowing sand or snow or where parts of the rock have crumbled away due to solution of the mineral cement that holds the sand grains together.

SHALE: Shale is formed by consolidation and compaction of clay. Clay, in turn, is composed largely of clay minerals formed by chemical decay of feldspars and other mineral grains during weathering or by reactions with hot underground water. Clay generally contains some silt, which is composed of very fine particles of quartz or other resistant minerals. Clay is transported for great distances by streams and ocean currents and deposited over much of the floor of the oceans or in stream terraces and deltas. Thus, shale is perhaps the most common of the sedimentary rocks. However, shale is rather easily eroded and for this reason shale alone does not generally form high mountains, but is widespread on the plains and in basins between the ranges. Nevertheless, shale interlayered with resistant sandstone forms a number of high peaks, including at least four of the Colorado Fourteeners.

Shale characteristically breaks into small, flat chips or platelets that make for slippery slopes and difficult walking. Where interlayered with sandstone, the shale forms benches and gentle (but treacherous) slopes between cliff bands formed by the more resistant sandstone. Shale can be black, gray, or green, but most commonly in the Colorado mountains it is red, maroon, or black.

One other problem that shale poses to mountain travelers is not so much in the mountains themselves, but on the approach to backcountry trailheads. Where unpaved dirt roads cross thick shale deposits, rain can quickly turn them into quagmires due to wetting of the clay minerals in the shale. As one of our U.S. Geological Survey colleagues, who had spent many years driving such roads, once remarked about the Mancos Shale (one of the most widespread shale formations): "The West would have been a better place if the #@*! Mancos had never been deposited!"

The #@*! Mancos shale near Green Mountain Reservoir.

LIMESTONE: Limestone is a chemically precipitated sedimentary rock composed largely of calcium carbonate (calcite) deposited as limey mud on the sea floor or locally in lakes. The carbonate can either be precipitated directly from the water, or it can accumulate in the form of fossil shells or other parts of water-dwelling organisms. In the climate of Colorado, limestone is relatively resistant to erosion and forms prominent cliffs and hogbacks. This is surprising to geologists who have worked in more humid climates like the Appalachians, where limestone commonly forms valleys and lowlands between resistant ridges of sandstone or other harder rocks.

Limestone is a fine-grained rather uniform rock that is commonly gray, but can be white, tan,

Limestone. Irregular fluted appearance of the outcrop surface is typical. Rock here is cut by thin veins of calcite. Some of the white areas are nodules of chert.

or brown. In many places it contains thin layers or irregular masses of silica (chert) that weather out on exposed faces to form rough but welcome handholds and footholds. It is generally cut by joints, many of which are approximately perpen-

Lauri Strickler attacks a layback crack in limestone along the Shelf Road in Garden Park near Cañon City. STEWART M. GREEN PHOTO

dicular to the sedimentary beds. These form chimneys and jam cracks and cause the rock to break into rectangular blocks of various sizes. These blocks form relatively stable talus.

Limestone occurs in many scattered areas in the Colorado mountains, but is not an important component of the high peaks. It does however offer spectacular rock climbing, notably in the areas of Garden Park near Cañon City and Rifle Mountain Park near Rifle. It also supports world-class ice climbs above Vail, and is well beloved by spelunkers because it hosts myriad spectacular caves.

DOLOMITE: A close relative of limestone is the rock dolomite, composed chiefly of the mineral dolomite (calcium-magnesium carbonate). It is almost indistinguishable from limestone except by a simple test used by geologists. If you place a drop of dilute hydrochloric acid on limestone it will fizz vigorously, but dolomite will only fizz if you scratch it or powder it. Dolomite is formed in the same way as limestone, or by alteration of limestone by mineral-bearing solutions.

IGNEOUS ROCKS

Igneous rocks are formed by cooling and solidification of molten or partly molten rock material in or on the Earth's crust. This material, called magma, is formed by fusion of parts of the crust. The melting can be driven by the rise of hot material from the upper part of the Earth's mantle; by introduction of volatile materials such as water, carbon dioxide or fluorine; or by decrease in pressure due to movement of tectonic plates. Magma is never completely a liquid—generally it consists of a "mush" of liquid, mineral crystals, and rock fragments. Most magmas are less dense than the surrounding rocks and tend to rise toward the surface. If they reach the surface they form lava flows or are erupted explosively as volcanic ash, cinders, pumice, or bombs. These are called volcanic rocks. Magmas that solidify before they reach the surface form plutonic rocks, which occur in a wide variety of sizes and shapes ranging from batholiths (many miles across) through stocks (several miles across) to plugs (a mile or so across). Smaller bodies include dikes (tabular bodies that cut across beds or layers in the enclosing rocks) and sills (tabular bodies that lie parallel to beds or layers in the enclosing rocks), which were injected into the surrounding country rocks.

Magmas have diverse compositions that depend on the composition of the rocks from which they formed and their history of cooling and crystallization. As magma cools, crystals of various minerals form and begin to grow at particular temperatures in a systematic sequence. It takes time for the atoms in the magma to organize themselves into orderly crystal edifices. Therefore, the size of the mineral grains gives an indication of how fast the magma cooled. If the cooling was rapid, as it is in most volcanic rocks, the mineral crystals are small; if it was slow, the crystals are larger, as they are in many plutonic rocks. The minerals that formed earlier commonly assume regular crystal shapes, but as crystallization continues the growing crystals interfere with one another and form irregular interlocking shapes.

Plutonic Rocks

Plutonic rocks are characterized by mineral grains that are easily visible to the naked eye or under a low-power magnifying glass, by the presence of recognizable crystals, and by the fact that they form bodies that cut across beds or layers in the enclosing rocks. By far the most common plutonic rock in the Colorado mountains is granite, but other plutonic rocks also play important roles in shaping the landscapes of many of the ranges.

GRANITE: Granite is a light-colored plutonic rock composed primarily of grains of feldspar and quartz, with smaller amounts of mica and/or hornblende. Geologists sometimes use the term "granite" to designate a rock with an especially high ratio of potassium feldspar to plagioclase feldspar, but here we use it in the more general sense for any plutonic rock in which quartz and feldspar occur in roughly equal proportions and mica and/or hornblende constitute only a small proportion of the rock.

Mineral grains in granite range in size from an inch or more to the size of a match-head. The feldspar crystals are typically more or less rectangular, light pink or white, and have smooth faces that glitter in the sun. Quartz is generally in smoky gray, irregular grains that do not have crystal faces. Muscovite (white mica) forms silvery gray shiny flakes; biotite (black mica) forms dark brown or black shiny flakes; and hornblende forms black or dark green grains shaped like tiny prisms. In some granite the grains are randomly arranged and the rock is massive and uniform. However, in many granites the grains are crudely aligned, giving the rock a streaky appearance. This streaky arrangement of minerals, called foliation, can be due to flow of the magma as it was crystallizing or to strain during later rock deformation.

Where granite has been recently scoured by glacial ice, it is smooth and polished, but where the rock has escaped recent glaciation, exposed granite faces are roughened by weathering so that larger and more resistant mineral grains project, producing a surface ideal for friction climbing.

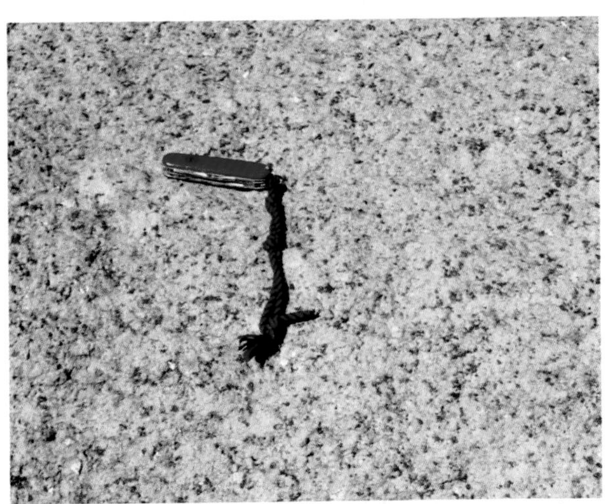

Granite. Gray, irregular grains are quartz, pink crystals are potassium feldspar, chalky white grains are plagioclase feldspar, and black grains are biotite. Some faces of potassium feldspar glitter in the sun.

Resistant blocks of other rocks frozen into the granite as it crystallized may project as knobs or nubbins, providing welcome holds. Typically, granite faces are broken by widely spaced joints of various orientations that provide a variety of chimneys, jam cracks, and layback cracks. Frost shattering has produced jumbles of huge joint-bounded blocks on the high ridges and summits of many granite peaks.

Foliated granite. Gray, irregular grains are quartz, both potassium feldspar and plagioclase are white, but potassium feldspar forms most of the larger crystals. Dark mineral is chiefly biotite. Foliation is produced by parallel arrangement of biotite-rich streaks and lens-shaped aggregates of quartz and feldspar. Where the foliation is strongly developed, the rock is sometimes called granite gneiss.

A climber's view of granite on the east face of Longs Peak.

In areas of deep weathering, joint-bounded blocks of granite tend to come apart in concentric sheets, like layers of an onion. This type of weathering, called exfoliation, produces smooth domes and rounded boulders that are typical of many granite areas. Long-continued weathering causes massive granite to break down into grus, a coarse loose soil made up of angular grains of feldspar and quartz, which is too porous to retain water. Dry grus-covered slopes in forests are particularly prone to wildfire—the Buffalo Creek (1996) and Hayman (2002) fires both raged through such areas.

Chemical decay of mineral grains and mechanical disintegration of granite produces domes, towers, and rounded boulders of granite and loose, sandy soil (grus). VAN WILLIAMS PHOTO

Because granite is relatively resistant to erosion, it forms more of Colorado's Fourteeners than any other type of rock. Granite's beauty, solidity, and general reliability have made this rock much beloved by generations of climbers.

PEGMATITE: Pegmatite is a close relative of granite. It is also composed chiefly of feldspar and quartz, with smaller amounts of biotite, muscovite, and other rarer minerals, but the individual mineral crystals are very large. Commonly the crystals are several inches in diameter; in some rare cases they are several feet across. Quartz generally appears as greasy gray, irregular streaks and lenses rather than well-formed crystals, but tabular crystals of

Dike of pegmatite cutting gneiss. Chief minerals are pink potassium feldspar, gray to milky white quartz, chalky white plagioclase, and black biotite.

feldspar and plate-like crystals of mica are conspicuous. Crystals of potassium feldspar are commonly pink and display small wormlike patterns on crystal faces; crystals of plagioclase feldspar are white or gray and their faces display a pattern of closely spaced parallel lines visible with a hand lens. The mica crystals can easily be separated into thin transparent sheets with a pocket knife. Pegmatite commonly also contains crystals of garnet, magnetite (magnetic iron oxide—check your compass!), and tourmaline. In a few areas, it contains rarer minerals much prized by collectors.

Pegmatite forms during the last phases of crystallization of granitic magma. As the magma forms and minerals crystallize, volatile components such as water, carbon dioxide, fluorine, and chlorine are concentrated into a water-rich fluid, which facilitates the growth of the large crystals. Pegmatite forms streaks, veins, and irregular masses a few inches to a few feet across in granite and in the surrounding rocks, especially in the metamorphic rocks in many of the Colorado Ranges. Commonly, these pegmatite bodies weather out to form fins, ledges, and knobs that offer felicitous holds and convenient routes on otherwise unpromising rock.

GABBRO: A dark-colored coarse-grained plutonic rock composed of pyroxene and plagioclase feldspar. Where the rock has been metamorphosed, the pyroxene is commonly converted to hornblende. Gabbro occurs among the basement rocks in several Colorado ranges, notably in the

Park Range, but forms high peaks only in the Sangre de Cristo Range, where it is an important part of the architecture of Blanca and its neighbors.

PORPHYRY: The name "porphyry" describes any igneous rock that contains large crystals scattered through a rock primarily composed of much smaller grains or crystals. However, among Colorado geologists it is used specifically to describe a group of rocks that is widespread in the Colorado mountains and which are important components of the Elk and West Elk Mountains. In this usage it describes a white, light-gray, light-green, or pink rock composed chiefly of very small crystals of feldspar and quartz (ranging in

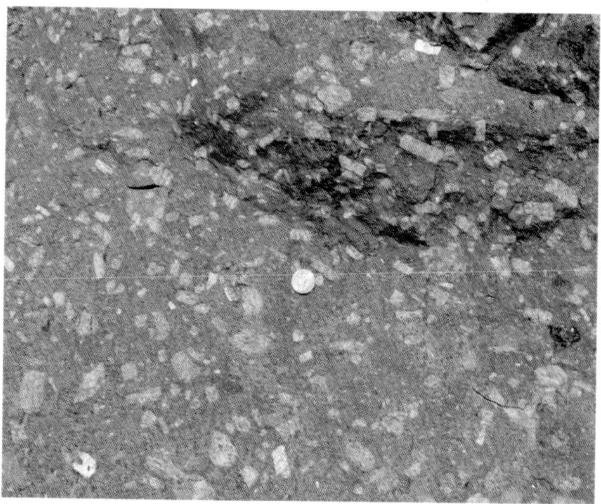

Porphyry. Large crystals are potassium feldspar, several of which are glistening in the sun. The finer part of the rock, called the groundmass, is composed of quartz, feldspar, and some biotite. The coin in the picture is a quarter.

size from smaller than grains of sugar to the size of match heads), and containing conspicuous larger crystals of feldspar and quartz. Porphyry forms stocks, plugs, and dikes in many types of rock; where it intrudes sedimentary rocks, it commonly forms sills and large flat-bottomed pillow-like bodies called laccoliths. Porphyry typically breaks up into small plates, blocks, and angular fragments. Where it occurs in large stocks and laccoliths, slopes are littered with unstable talus and festooned with rock glaciers (glacier-like streams of talus that contain ice between the blocks and move slowly downslope). Walking on these slopes is unpleasant at best, and scrambling or technical climbing on porphyry is definitely to be avoided!

Volcanic rocks

Volcanic rocks are very widespread in the Colorado mountains, but only in the San Juan Mountains do they constitute the dominant rocks in a major range. They include a wide and confusing variety of rocks of differing compositions and origins, some of which can be distinguished only by microscopic study and laboratory analysis. These rocks include lava flows, formed by solidification of magma that flows out on the surface, and pyroclastic rocks, formed from material that was explosively ejected into the atmosphere. They also include material that was carried off the flanks of volcanoes by floods, mud slides, and debris flows, then deposited in surrounding valleys and lowlands.

BASALT: Basalt is probably the volcanic rock best known to the general public. It is also the most common volcanic rock on Earth, because it forms the floors of all of the oceans and large lava fields on most of the continents. In Colorado, basalt flows cap buttes and mesas such as the Table Mountains near Golden, the Grand Mesa, and the Flattops, but nowhere does basalt form high peaks. Thus, it is of little interest to peak baggers, but it furnishes technical rock climbers with a variety of challenging practice climbs.

Basalt is a heavy dark-gray or greenish gray rock that is made up principally of plagioclase

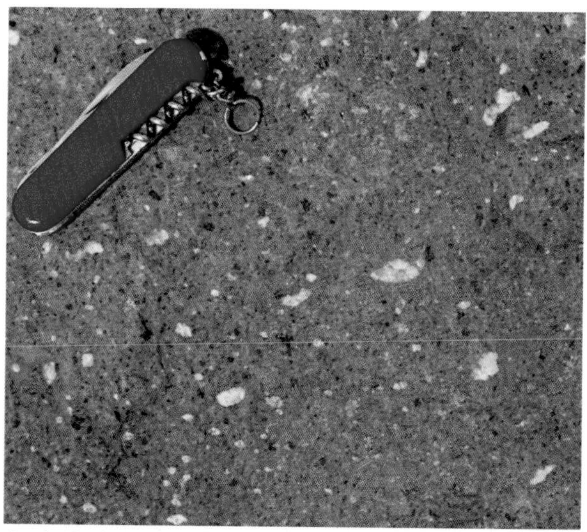

Basalt. The gray material that makes up most of the rock is composed of very small crystals of plagioclase feldspar and pyroxene (too small to distinguish in the photo). Dark spots are larger crystals of pyroxene. White oval areas are gas bubbles in the lava that were subsequently filled with quartz and other minerals.

feldspar and dark green pyroxene. The rock is generally too fine grained to recognize individual mineral grains, but commonly a few larger tabular crystals of white or gray plagioclase or dark-green pyroxene are visible with a hand lens. Basalt commonly contains spherical or ovoid cavities formed by gas bubbles trapped as the lava solidified.

Basalt flows are generally a few feet to several hundred feet thick and form conspicuous cliff bands. On slopes where several flows are superimposed they are marked by a series of cliff bands separated by benches formed by erosion of softer sedimentary rocks between them. One of the characteristic features of lava flows, and particu-

Climbing on basalt. The vertical joints outline six-sided columns. Part of the column on the left has broken away, leaving the overhanging roof above the climber in the yellow helmet. The horizontal joints, like the one on which the climber in the white helmet is standing, are perpendicular to the columns and approximately parallel to the surface of the lava flow. BOB PEARSON PHOTO

larly of basalt flows, is the development of a series of joints perpendicular to the flow surface that cause the rocks to separate into polygonal columns like those so often seen in photographs of the Devils Postpile in California or the Giant's Causeway in Ireland. The joints, called columnar jointing, form as the lava contracts slightly as it cools and crystallizes, much like the cracks that form when mud dries and contracts. The cracks between the columns form regularly spaced narrow chimneys and jam or layback cracks. Another set of joints commonly lies perpendicular to the columns, forming finger and toe holds on the faces, and belay ledges where columns break off during erosion.

TUFF: During explosive volcanic eruptions great volumes of volcanic ash are expelled into the air, rising in giant, billowing clouds, sometimes to the base of the stratosphere. The "ash" is not really produced by anything burning. It is composed of fine shards of volcanic glass formed by shattering of small bubbles produced by sudden release of gases in the magma as it reaches the surface, much like the foam produced when you open a can of beer, thus releasing the pressure. Tuff is the rock that is formed by consolidation of volcanic ash. The ash can travel hundreds, even thousands, of miles, but eventually most of it drifts gently down to form a loose deposit that may eventually consolidate as air fall tuff. Such deposits are interesting and often scenic, but they are generally not significant components of the mountain landscape.

In large eruptions, particularly of gas-saturated lava rich in silica, parts of the eruption cloud may collapse to form turbulent high-speed avalanches of incandescent ash, rock fragments, and superheated gas. These avalanches, sometimes referred to as *nuees ardentes* (French for glowing clouds), may have temperatures as high as 1500°F and can travel at speeds greater than a hundred miles per hour for many miles. They generally follow valleys, but large high-velocity flows have been known to overtop saddles and ridges hundreds of feet above the valley floors.

When one of these glowing avalanches finally comes to rest, much of the glassy ash is still so hot that it welds together and forms a fine-grained rock called welded tuff. Layers of welded

The eruption of Mount St. Helens on May 18, 1980, spread ash over vast areas, even coating the windshields of cars as far away as Denver. U.S. GEOLOGICAL SURVEY PHOTO

tuff range from a few feet to hundreds of feet thick. Commonly, the upper part of each layer is only loosely welded, but the lower parts are completely welded into a dense hard rock, and the base of the deposit may be marked by a layer of obsidian (black volcanic glass).

Welded tuff is generally white, light-gray, yellow, or tan fine-grained rock that somewhat resembles sandstone at first glance. Commonly, it contains flattened, darker colored fragments of frothy volcanic rock, and in many places flattened fragments of volcanic glass give the rock a wormy texture visible with careful study under a hand lens. This texture, plus the fact that welded tuff commonly displays columnar jointing, help distinguish it from sandstone. Sheets of welded tuff form resistant ledges and cap buttes and mesas in several Colorado Ranges, especially in large parts of the eastern San Juans.

Welded tuff. The bulk of this rock is composed of welded shards of volcanic glass, with a few small crystals of clear quartz and white feldspar scattered throughout. Angular fragments of other ejecta from the eruption cloud are commonly found, but none is visible in the photo. Coin in the photo is a dime.

VOLCANIC BRECCIA: Breccia is any rock made up of angular pieces of older rocks cemented together by finer grained material. Breccia can form in many ways, including breakup of rocks along faults, collapse of caves, and cementation of talus or rockfalls. However, the most widespread breccia in the Colorado mountains formed during volcanic eruptions. Volcanic breccia is composed of angular broken fragments, chiefly of volcanic rocks, set in a matrix composed chiefly of volcanic ash or small sand-sized fragments of volcanic rocks. Most of the large rock fragments are a foot or less in diameter, but some breccia contains

Tuff layers exposed at the Wheeler Geologic Area near Creede. Light colored material in the lower half of the picture is non-welded tuff. The darker layer in the middle of the picture is welded tuff at the base of the next ash flow. It grades upward into gray non-welded tuff. The thin white layer at the base of the dark layer is non-welded tuff composed of material that was blown by supersonic shock waves generated by the explosion that accompanied the eruption of the upper ash flow.

larger fragments, ten feet or more across. Volcanic breccia is generally gray, purplish gray, or tan, but where it has been altered by mineral-bearing solutions it assumes a vivid array of colors, including yellow, orange, vermillion, and brown.

Volcanic breccia can form by collapse of the flanks of a volcano, by breaking up of solidified crust on the tops of lava flows, and in a number of other ways, but most commonly it represents material carried down by violent mudflows triggered by heavy rains or by melting of glaciers or snowfields during volcanic eruptions. These mudflows can travel many miles and spread large aprons of volcanic debris in the lowlands surrounding the volcano. Commonly, many of the

Volcanic breccia. Note that the blocks are all angular and that they consist of a variety of rock types including welded tuff and dark lava. This breccia was probably deposited as a mudflow.

fragments in these mudflows are rounded pebbles, cobbles, or boulders, and the rock shows characteristics of both breccia and conglomerate, but we include it here with the volcanic rocks because it is composed largely of volcanic materials. Volcanic breccia and conglomerate are widespread in the San Juan and West Elk Mountains. Where they are not strongly cemented they erode into spectacular badlands with near-vertical pinnacles or columns, commonly with loose rock and tempting but unreliable holds. Where they are more firmly

Thick layers of volcanic breccia and conglomerate near Wolf Creek Pass.

cemented, they form broken cliffs and steep-walled canyons. In general, volcanic breccia and conglomerate form unstable slopes, extensive talus, and make for difficult off-trail traveling, but where they are well cemented, erosion-roughened faces and projecting rock fragments offer inviting scrambling and technical climbing.

METAMORPHIC ROCKS

When you bake a cake, you mix various ingredients, including flour, eggs, shortening, and yeast, and heat the mixture enough that the ingredients react chemically with one another to form a new material, one in which you can no longer identify the original ingredients. If you don't bake it long enough or hot enough, the ingredients don't react completely and the cake isn't done; if you bake it too long or at too high a temperature you get a different result, a burned cake. If you are a newcomer to Colorado, you soon learn that the proper baking time and temperature depend on the altitude, that is, on the atmospheric pressure.

So it is with rocks. If you take a mixture of mineral grains—say a sedimentary rock that has formed at the earth's surface—and heat it hot enough and long enough, the mineral grains will react with one another to form new minerals. The reactions that take place and the minerals that are formed depend not only on the temperature and time of heating, but also on the pressure. The reaction of mineral grains in response to changes in temperature and pressure is called metamorphism, and the rocks formed in this way are metamorphic rocks. Igneous rocks can also be metamorphosed, but because their mineral grains formed at high temperatures, reactions between them generally produce minerals that are stable together at lower temperatures than those that prevailed when the rock originally formed.

There are two ways in which metamorphic rocks form. One is by burial within the crust at depths where temperatures and pressures are high enough to drive chemical reactions between the mineral grains. This generally happens where tectonic plates collide and one plate is forced under the other. Because this typically involves large volumes of rock over broad areas it is described as regional metamorphism. The other way that metamorphic rocks form is by heating of the wall rocks along the margins of hot bodies of magma. This is called contact metamorphism. Both types of metamorphic rocks are found in the Colorado mountains, but regional metamorphic rocks are by far the most extensive. They form the cores of several of the major ranges, whereas contact metamorphic rocks are significant only locally in a few ranges. The principal types of metamorphic rocks in the Colorado mountains are schist, gneiss, and amphibolite, which are regional metamorphic rocks, and hornfels, which is a contact metamorphic rock.

SCHIST: Schist is produced by regional metamorphism of shale. It is a medium- or coarse-grained rock composed chiefly of mica, quartz, and feldspar that takes its name from its principal characteristic, schistosity. Schistosity is the parallel arrangement of the mica flakes that gives the rock a sheeted appearance and causes it to split into shiny flakes and thin slabs. The quartz and feldspar form thin lenses or knots that are flattened parallel to the mica flakes. Close examination of a surface parallel to the plane of schistosity commonly shows that the minerals are arranged in linear streaks on the surface as a result of movement along the planes during metamorphism. Schist is generally various shades of gray and appears silvery where broken parallel to the schistosity because of the shiny surfaces of the mica flakes.

Schist. The surface of the rock in this picture is parallel to the planes of schistosity. The most conspicuous minerals are biotite (black), muscovite (silvery white), feldspar (chalky white), and quartz (glassy gray). However, another important mineral in this particular schist is fibrous white sillimanite (Al_2Si0_2); the presence of sillimanite indicates that this rock was metamorphosed at a depth of more than seven miles and at temperatures of more than 900°F!

Schist is fairly resistant to erosion and tends to form bold cliffs and prominent rugged ridges. It is commonly broken by joints perpendicular to the schistosity. Often one set of these joints is perpendicular to the mineral streaking on the planes of schistosity—these are called cross joints. The "climbability" of schist depends strongly on the orientation of the schistosity. Faces parallel to the schistosity are embellished with small nubbins and friction holds where quartz and feldspar knots project because of weathering of the softer mica. Faces that cut across the schistosity are

Delicate footwork on a rock face nearly parallel to the schistosity.
KAY MILLER PHOTO

commonly roughened by the projecting edges of the planes of schistosity that form small ledges and fingerholds. Schist is very commonly laced with dikes and irregular bodies of pegmatite that tend to project as knobs or fins on weathered surfaces and add variety to many climbing routes.

One unpleasant feature of schist is the tendency of thin slabs to flake off unexpectedly, sometimes with consequences that can ruin your day. Because of the way it breaks into chips and slabs, schist forms talus and scree that are unstable and slippery, especially when wet. We discov-

Muscling up a rock face perpendicular to the schistosity. KAY MILLER PHOTO

ered one redeeming feature of traveling over schist at night on a descent of Chief Mountain a few years ago. The beams of our headlamps reflecting off the large mica flakes in the schist gave the marvelous feeling of walking in a crystal fairyland!

GNEISS: Gneiss (pronounced "nice") is a general term for a metamorphic rock in which alternating light and dark layers, or lenses, give the rock an irregular banded or streaky appearance. This definition covers a wide variety of rocks of different compositions and origins. Several types of gneiss are common among the regional metamorphic rocks in the Colorado mountains.

One type, mica gneiss, is a medium- to dark-gray rock composed of feldspar, quartz, and mica (chiefly biotite). The mineral grains are small, ranging in size from grains of sugar to the size of BBs; and the lighter and darker layers contain different proportions of biotite. The mica flakes are generally aligned parallel to the layers, but the rock contains too little mica to develop schistosity so it tends to break in rectangular blocks instead of coming apart in chips and slabs like schist. Mica gneiss commonly occurs intimately interleaved with schist and is probably formed by metamorphism of sandy layers in the shale from which the schist was formed. Mica gneiss is generally more resistant to erosion than schist, so where it is interlayered with schist it forms more continuous cliffs and ledges of sounder rock broken by more regularly spaced joints.

Another common type of gneiss is felsic gneiss, a sugary textured rock composed almost entirely of feldspar and quartz, with only minor amounts of biotite. Felsic gneiss is generally white, light gray, or tan, and displays layers a few inches to many feet thick that differ in color because they contain greater or lesser amounts of biotite or hornblende. Felsic gneiss is commonly interleaved with discontinuous layers or lenses of amphibolite, a dark-green to almost black rock composed almost entirely of plagioclase feldspar and hornblende. Amphibolite is so named because hornblende belongs to a family of minerals called amphiboles. The felsic gneiss was formed by

Mica gneiss. Chief difference from felsic gneiss is the increased amount of biotite, which gives the rock a light- to medium-gray color. The biotite is arranged in wispy aggregates that give the rock a streaky appearance. Coin in the photo is a quarter.

metamorphism of silica-rich volcanic rocks like welded tuff, whereas the amphibolite represents metamorphosed flows or dikes of basalt.

Felsic gneiss typically forms bold cliffs broken by many continuous joints. Layers in the gneiss are commonly contorted into complex folds a few inches to many feet across. The diversity of rocks, the contortion of the layers, and an abundance of dikes and pods of resistant pegmatite cutting through the layers give many cliff faces the appearance of a chaotic geological tapestry. The layers and pods of rock of different composition weather at different rates, so faces that cut across the layering are typically broken by numerous

Felsic gneiss (light-colored rock) interlayered with amphibolite (dark rock). The amphibolite layers range from a few inches to thousands of feet thick.

small ledges and projections where the more resistant rocks protrude. Faces parallel with the layering generally have fewer holds and require more challenging friction climbing. As with most layered rocks, the character of the climbing depends on the orientation of the rock face relative to the layering. If the layering slopes into the face, holds are larger and more trustworthy; where it slopes out of the rock face, holds are fewer and less secure. Felsic gneiss and its interlayered amphibolite generally form blocky, angular talus that is relatively stable, except on very steep rocky slopes with outward-sloping layers.

MIGMATITE: Like all classifications of natural things, classification of rocks into simple sedimentary, igneous, and metamorphic categories sometime runs into inconvenient cases that don't

Migmatite. Lighter colored areas have the composition of granite (essentially quartz and feldspar). Dark areas are biotite gneiss and schist. White ruler is about 8 inches long.

fit neatly into a single category. Migmatite (literally "mixed rock") is one of these. It is composed of a mixture of metamorphic rock and igneous rock. It takes many forms, but the most common one in Colorado is a mixture of biotite schist or gneiss and granite. This type of migmatite consists of dark biotite-rich streaks, lenses or discontinuous layers fractions of an inch to several inches thick, alternating with thin irregular pods, layers, and streaks of lighter colored granite that make up as much as half of the total rock. Commonly the layers and lenses are complexly folded into patterns resembling the streaks in soft taffy. If you heat a rock composed of quartz, feldspar, and biotite, such as biotite gneiss or schist, the quartz and feldspar tend to melt first, forming a liquid with a composition like granite. In most places the granitic parts of the migmatite were

Beds of quartzite in the Sawatch Range. Individual beds are a few inches to several feet thick.

probably formed by this type of partial melting at very high temperature and pressure. However, it is also possible that some of the granite material in the migmatite was injected into the gneiss from nearby plutonic bodies of granite.

QUARTZITE: Quartzite is a hard, sugary textured or glassy rock consisting largely of recrystallized quartz that is formed by regional metamorphism of sandstone. It is generally white, light gray, or bluish gray. Commonly, it contains scattered pebbles and may contain layers of metamorphosed conglomerate. Quartzite is not common in most Colorado Ranges, but it forms the spectacular peaks of the Grenadier Range in the Needle Mountains, where the firm rock and soaring faces furnish some of the finest climbing in the Colorado mountains.

Climbing on the face of a bedding plane in quartzite. Climber is depending on small finger and toe holds formed where joints cut the bedding. HARLAN BARTON PHOTO

HORNFELS: Hornfels is a very hard, dark, fine-grained rock that is formed from contact metamorphism of shale adjacent to intrusions of granite, porphyry, or other igneous rocks. It is relatively resistant to erosion and forms jagged ridges and cliffs. It breaks into sharp, angular fragments that form loose, treacherous talus and scree. Fortunately it forms the summits of only a handful of the high peaks. It has few positive attributes to recommend it to technical rock climbers and is best avoided except by the most devoted peak baggers.

TWO

The Rocks Remember

Geologic Time as Revealed in Colorado's Rocks

"What seest thou else
In the dark backwards and abysm of time?"
WILLIAM SHAKESPEARE
The Tempest, Act 1, Scene 2

The complex tapestry of different ages and types of rocks in the Colorado mountains seems almost random, yet if we study the rocks carefully and try to decipher their individual stories we find that they record a fascinating chronicle of geologic events beginning almost 2 billion years ago and still continuing today. These tales tell of the slow shift of continents, the rise and destruction of mountain ranges, the ebb and flow of ancient seas, and the work of wind, water, and glacial ice in shaping the ever-changing landscape.

To visualize the enormous span of time involved, it may help to picture an ordinary yardstick as representing the 4.5 billion years that have elapsed from the time the Earth and the other planets accumulated from the dust of an exploding star to the present. On this yardstick of time, each inch represents 125 million years. On this scale, the dinosaurs evolved, flourished, and died between 2 inches and one-half inch from the present (250 and 64 million

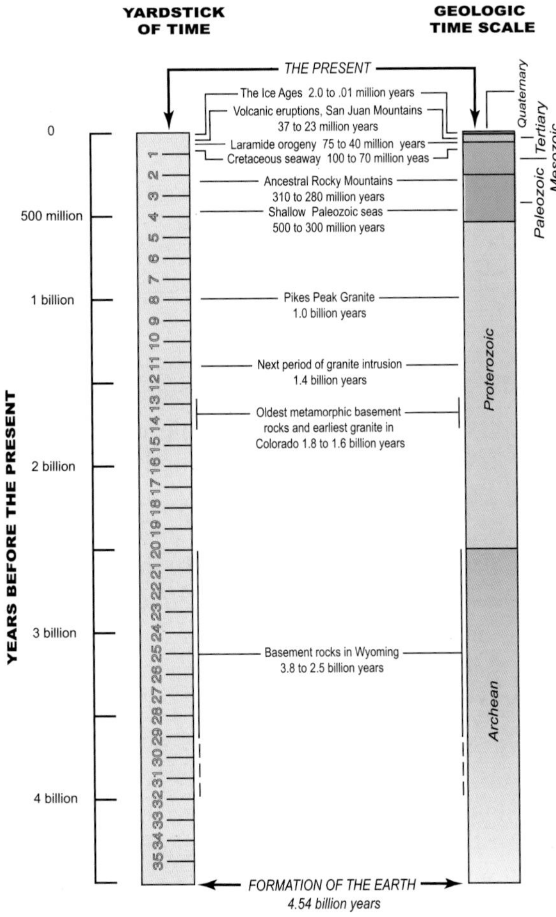

The yardstick of geologic time.

years ago). Modern humans have inhabited the Earth for about the last 2 million years, a length of time that would be represented by the thickness of four sheets of paper at the top of our yardstick.

The part of the story recorded in Colorado's rocks begins about 1.8 billion years ago (about 14½ inches from the top of our yardstick) with the accumulation of thick deposits of volcanic and sedimentary rocks in and between chains of volcanic islands, perhaps much like the volcano-studded islands of modern Indonesia. These island chains lay offshore of an ancient continent whose edge was in what is now southern Wyoming. The island chains were part of tectonic plates that were moving northward (in modern coordinates) as the ocean floor on which they rode was being forced down and under the edge of the continent. As the island chains encountered the edge of the old continent they were stripped off the down-going ocean floor and plastered against the southern continental margin. During the complicated dance of tectonic plates, much of the accumulated sediment and volcanic debris was carried down to depths as much as eight or ten miles below the surface.

Millions and Billions

A million is a thousand thousand (1,000,000) or in scientific notation 1×10^6; a billion is a thousand million (1,000,000,000) or in scientific notation 1×10^9. One million dimes would make a stack 0.8 mile high; a billion dimes would make a stack 800 miles high. This should give a feel for both the length of geologic time and the size of the federal budget.

About 1.7 billion years ago, these deeply buried rocks were invaded by large masses of hot magma, some of which fed volcanoes at the surface, and some of which crystallized at depth to form granite and other plutonic rocks. The heat and pressure of deep burial and igneous intrusion converted the original sediments and volcanic materials into the gneiss, schist, and other metamorphic rocks now exposed in the eroded cores of many of the modern mountain ranges and in most of the deeper canyons. Twice more these ancient metamorphic rocks were injected by large bodies of magma: once about 1.4 billion years ago and once about 1.1 billion years ago. The first of these episodes produced large, irregular bodies of granite and swarms of pegmatite dikes that crisscross the metamorphic rocks wherever they are exposed; the second episode produced the great mass of granite and gem-bearing pegmatite that now makes up Pikes Peak.

The ancient metamorphic and igneous rocks are commonly referred to as "basement rocks", because they lie beneath all younger sedimentary rocks. The details of their story are vague. Some we are only beginning to understand; some we will never know. We do know that in the long interval of time between the emplacement of the Pikes Peak Granite and the beginning of the Paleozoic Era about 540 million years ago (about 4¼ inches on the yardstick) any pre-existing mountain uplifts were deeply eroded, and the basement rocks that had lain many miles below the Earth's surface were once again exposed, forming a subdued landscape of low, rounded hills and shallow valleys. About 500 million years ago, shallow, tropical seas began to flood eastward across the continent. For the next 200 million years, sand and mud sweeping into this seaway built up layer upon layer of sandstone and shale while calcium carbonate from shells and skeletons of marine organisms formed extensive layers of limestone. Eventually, these sedimentary deposits reached a combined thickness of a few hundred to a thousand feet or more. We see them grandly exposed today in Glenwood Canyon, along the western flank of the Sawatch Range, the east flank of the Front Range near Colorado Springs, and capping some of the highest peaks in the Tenmile and Mosquito Ranges.

The long period of quiescence during which this blanket of sedimentary rocks was deposited ended

Lower Paleozoic strata exposed in Glenwood Canyon. Dashed yellow line indicates the base of the basal Paleozoic formation, Sawatch Quartzite. Beneath the line the rock is 1.7 billion-year-old granite. Geologists refer to this as the "Great Unconformity".

about 320 million years ago (about 2½ inches on the yardstick) when plate tectonic movements brought the southern part of North America in contact with South America and Africa. The contact could hardly be described as a collision—it took place at about the same rate that your fingernails grow. Nevertheless enormous forces raised and faulted great mountain blocks in what is now Texas, Oklahoma, New Mexico, Colorado, and parts of Wyoming and Utah. Only the eroded cores of these Ancestral Rocky Mountains remain, even though they may once have towered as high or higher than our present mountains. The record of their former grandeur lies in great thicknesses of red sandstone and conglomerate formed from erosion of these ancient, lofty peaks. These strata are now exposed along the Front Range in the Flatirons, Red Rocks, and Garden of the Gods, in the Maroon Bells of the Elk Mountains, in Crestone Peak and Crestone Needle in the northern Sangre de Cristo Range, and on the flanks of the San Juan Mountains.

As the ancient ranges rose, the earlier sedimentary formations were eroded from the uplifts exposing the underlying basement rocks. The positions of the former ranges are now marked by areas where the older sedimentary rocks are absent and the red sandstones and conglomerates or younger strata rest directly on the basement rocks. In Colorado there were two major ranges of the Ancestral Rocky Mountains. One lay approximately in the position of the present Front Range, extending south from Wyoming and southeast into New Mexico; the other was in the general area of the Uncompahgre Plateau, but much broader, extending southeast from Utah through the present site of the San Juan Mountains. The uplift of these ranges continued for perhaps 70 million years. As the mountains rose, weathering and erosion shaped the peaks and carved their valleys; when uplift ceased, these processes continued unabated, gradually reducing the peaks, first to low hills and finally to a near-level plain. Across this plain meandered sluggish, muddy rivers that were flanked by swamps in which a variety of dinosaurs flourished. Their bones are magnificently displayed in the fossil quarry at Dinosaur National Monument and on Dinosaur Ridge near Denver.

About 100 million years ago (about ⅞ of an inch on the yardstick), the sea once more spread across Colorado—this time advancing from northeast to southwest. As the shoreline advanced, beaches and sand bars coalesced to form a widespread deposit of white sand that we know as the Dakota Sandstone. Farther offshore, thick deposits of dark-gray silt and mud accumulated, swept into the sea by rivers flowing from the west. When the sea withdrew for the last time, about 70 million years ago, layers of sandstone and shale as much as two miles thick blanketed the eroded stumps of the Ancestral Rocky Mountain uplifts. The stage was set for the Laramide orogeny, the mountain-building episode that helped outline the present ranges of the Rocky Mountains. (Geologists love fancy words and *orogeny* is one of our favorites! It simply means a period of mountain building.)

Meanwhile, complicated interactions had been taking place for several hundred million years between western North America and various crustal plates in the Pacific Ocean. Mountain ranges rose and chains of volcanoes erupted as oceanic crust slid eastward beneath the continent, gradually sinking and partially melting beneath the North American continent. About 75 million years ago, the rate of plate convergence increased and deformation spread eastward and began to affect the area of the present Colorado mountains. The continental crust, weakened by heat from the slab of oceanic material that was sliding beneath it, began to buckle and shorten like an accordion, producing a series of great uplifts and downwarps in which the long-buried basement rocks were elevated or depressed thousands of feet from their former levels. Some of these uplifts were simple domes, some were elongated folds, and most were bounded by folds or faults along which slabs of rock were moved several miles with respect to the rocks beneath them. Though the details of how these structures developed have been debated by generations of geologists, the net result has been that the continental crust between Grand Junction and Denver has been shortened by some twenty-five to fifty miles, and the resulting uplifts became the sites of most of the major mountain ranges. Some of these uplifts rose at about the same places as the uplifts of the Ancestral Rocky Mountains. Others formed between or on the flanks of the older uplifts.

The Laramide orogeny lasted perhaps 30 million years—a geologically brief period. Individual uplifts, however, probably rose at rates of only a few inches per century (about one hundredth of the growth rate of your fingernails). As the rising uplifts were dissected by erosion, successive layers of sedimentary rocks were stripped away and the resistant basement rocks beneath were exposed. Material eroded from the rising uplifts accumulated in flanking basins and spread outward as extensive fans of sediment across the plains to the east. Uplift associated with the Laramide orogeny ended about 45 million years ago, but erosion continued. By about 35 million years ago (about ⅜ inch on the yardstick) the Laramide mountains were a series of hills and low, isolated mountains that stood above a rolling plain, most of which was only a few thousand feet above sea level. Remnants of this erosion surface are the oldest record of the history of the present mountains that are preserved in the modern landscape.

As the Laramide uplifts rose, masses of magma, perhaps generated by heat from the east-moving slab beneath the continent, began to rise through the Earth's crust. The magma bodies were injected in a

A reminder of a miner's world. The Champion Mill near Independence Pass in the Sawatch Range.

narrow belt that trends northeastward across Colorado from the southwestern San Juans to the Front Range northwest of Boulder. Many magma bodies solidified at depth, forming masses of granite or porphyry; others vented to the surface and fed volcanoes; some undoubtedly did both. The narrow northeast-trending belt of igneous rocks is known as the Colorado Mineral Belt because it contains almost all of the enormous deposits of gold, silver, lead, and zinc that supported the great Colorado mining districts of the late nineteenth and early twentieth centuries.

Mining in the Mountains

The history of mining in Colorado is long and interesting. Although the vast majority of Coloradans today earn their livelihoods through manufacturing, service industries, and agriculture, there were times in the not-too-distant past when the mining industry was a major employer. As you drive through the mountains you cannot help but notice the many disused dirt roads snaking improbably up steep slopes, the picturesque wooden mine buildings next to rusty head frames, and the piles of multicolored tailings along the sides of valleys.

Despite the old adage that "gold is where you find it", which seems to imply that the locations of mineral deposits might be somewhat random, these deposits and the mines that exploited them are located in specific places due to geologic factors that can be studied and to some extent predicted. Knowledge of these geologic factors and examination of how they might or might not apply to the terrain through which you are traveling can add to your understanding and appreciation of our spectacular countryside. And maybe, just maybe, such understanding will encourage you to keep your eyes peeled for some gold nuggets that were overlooked by those grizzled prospectors of yesteryear. However, you should be aware that those old geezers were nothing if not thorough. It is truly humbling to be hiking at 13,000 feet and stumble upon an old prospect hole hacked out by hand many miles from the nearest town. As you huff and puff carrying your pack filled with the lightest technical gear made of space-age fabrics and alloys, spare a few thoughts for the old sourdough who swung his heavy pick and shovel while subsisting on pork-and-beans and rotgut coffee.

As much as you notice where the old mines are located, you will probably also notice where they are not. Specific types of mineral deposits are generally located in specific areas, whereas other, nearby areas might have few or no similar deposits. In other words, some areas have been "blessed" by geologic factors that led to economically valuable mineral deposits, whereas other areas are "barren" of such deposits. For example, if you want to find coal, you would be well advised to look somewhere other than on the mountains around Breckenridge. The sedimentary environments in which the deposit of organic matter leads to the development of peat beds and eventually—after much burial and modification by heat and pressure—to the formation of coal just did not occur in the rocks now found around Breckenridge. If you're looking for deposits of metallic minerals such as gold and silver ores, however, then these mountains might be just the place to search. There is a fairly wide swath of territory extending from the San Juan Mountains northeastward to the Front Range that is known as the Colorado Mineral Belt due to the many rich ore deposits found there.

So what might lead you to suspect that the area through which you are hiking could be the location of unusual mineral deposits? An unexpected change in the colors of the rocks can be a clue to some types of mineral deposits. If you've been walking all day on large, dull gray blocks of granite and you suddenly stumble across broken, reddish brown blocks, you might be crossing a zone of rocks that were altered by hydrothermal (wet and hot) solutions. Many deposits of metallic minerals were formed from hydrothermal solutions that welled up through fault zones in pre-existing rocks and dumped their loads of dissolved metals and other elements when they encountered a change in chemical environments. These hot solutions changed not only the chemical composition of the rocks but also their colors, which was often the clue that prospectors looked for as they searched the hills for gold and glory.

As you trudge past an old mine site, you might want to stop for a few minutes and look at some of the waste rock that was produced as a byproduct of the mining activities. As the miners followed the ore veins, which were often quite narrow, they had to remove enough rock to allow them access and working room. Much of the rock that was removed—in fact probably most of it—did not contain economically valuable ore and was not worth milling, but was instead discarded outside the mine where it accumulated in what are known as tailings piles. Although most of the material in these piles is indeed waste rock and probably of little interest to the aspiring geologist, there are inevitably some pieces of ore mixed in. If you need an excuse to take a breather after that last uphill struggle, wander across the tailings and check out that dark-brown block half-buried in the loose yellowish tailings. Does it have any glints of metallic minerals? Break it open, and look at the unweathered inside. No need to use a hammer; simply smash it against another block of solid rock. Geologists always like to see the unweathered inside of a rock specimen because the weathering of the outside surface can remove some minerals and conceal others. You'll be surprised how many minerals can be found on an old tailings pile.

Some of the ore minerals that you are likely to find in the waste rock are pyrite (iron sulfide, also known as fool's gold), which occurs as yellow metallic grains; galena (lead sulfide), which occurs as gray metallic grains; and chalcopyrite (copper-iron sulfide), which occurs as coppery-red to yellow metallic grains. All of these ore minerals were mined in Colorado, not for those particular minerals themselves but rather because in some places they contained significant amounts of valuable gold and silver. The prospector knew to look for these common minerals because even if they did not themselves contain much gold or silver, they might indicate that more valuable ores were located nearby in rocks altered by the same hydrothermal solutions that produced the more common, but less valuable, indicator minerals.

We would caution you, however, never to enter old mines or pits, as they contain many dangers, including unstable rock, deep shafts, and deadly gases. You will probably see water flowing out of some old mines; this water is known as mine drainage or, in many cases, as acid mine drainage. Water flowing through mines commonly comes into contact with ore minerals and subsequently becomes more acidic and picks up various chemical compounds, which it carries out of the mine and into the nearby streams. Some of these streams have been stained reddish or yellowish for a distance downstream from the mine.

There is another, very practical reason for knowing something about the mining history of an area. You can expect an area that was heavily mined to have numerous access roads and trails. Although such roads might be too rugged and steep for use by modern passenger vehicles or even by four-wheel-drive SUVs, they are commonly ideal for the hiker. These old roads were usually built for horses and wagons, so their grades are gentle enough to provide easy access to many areas where, without these roads, the poor hiker would be thrashing through overgrown alders or high-stepping along a boulder-strewn hillside. More than a few hikers have learned to their advantage that three miles of winding mine road is often far easier to travel than a single mile of cross-country bushwhacking, if both routes get them to the same destination.

Igneous activity dwindled during the later stages of the Laramide orogeny, but after the orogeny and during the formation of the widespread erosion surface, it resumed and intensified. The most complete and impressive record is in the San Juan Mountains where between 35 and 26 million years ago dozens of volcanoes erupted thousands of feet of lava, volcanic breccia, and volcanic ash. Eventually, huge depressions ringed with volcanoes erupted hundreds of cubic miles of incandescent volcanic ash in clouds that surged outward for fifty miles or more. As the glowing ash settled out of the eruption clouds, it welded together under its own weight to form thick layers of hard, welded tuff so conspicuous in many of the peaks and canyons of the San Juans. Volcanoes also erupted during this interval in many other areas, including the West Elk Mountains and the Never Summer Range. Volcanic debris from South Park dammed streams flowing on the flat post-Laramide land surface, ponding a lake in which the beautifully preserved fossil leaves and insects were entombed at Florissant Fossil Beds National Monument near Cripple Creek.

At about the same time, great masses of igneous rocks which may or may not have vented to the surface were intruded in many ranges. These include large bodies of granite now exposed in the Sawatch Range, the San Miguel Mountains, the Elk and West Elk Mountains, and parts of the Front Range. Post-Laramide igneous rocks also added to the mineral wealth of the Colorado Mineral Belt and, more sparingly, to mineral deposits elsewhere. Intrusions of this age were responsible for the huge molybdenum deposits at the Henderson mine, the Climax mine, and Mt. Emmons.

The latest major episode in shaping the present mountain landscape began about 26 million years ago. Plate tectonic interactions along the western edge of the continent, which had caused shortening of the Earth's crust during the Laramide orogeny, changed so that much of western North America began to pull apart. The extension had two major effects in the area of the Colorado mountains. First, the land surface that developed after the Laramide orogeny and the volcanic rocks that were erupted on it were displaced by faults. Some parts of the surface were elevated, some were dropped down, and many parts were tilted. Most noteworthy of these fault breaks is the down-dropped block known as the Rio Grande rift, marked by the San Luis Valley—between the Sangre de Cristo and San Juan Mountains—and the upper Arkansas valley between the Sawatch and Mosquito Ranges. The second effect of the extension of the Earth's crust was that the entire region, which had lain only a few thousand feet above sea level, was elevated six thousand feet or more, probably as the result of increased flow of heat from great depths beneath the surface. As faulting and uplift proceeded, erosion by wind and water—and later by glaciers—carved the present landscape, shaping the present peaks and ranges and incising the major canyons. The hard basement rocks in the cores of the old Laramide uplifts, the thick layers of hard sandstone and conglomerate on their flanks, and the intrusive bodies of hard granite were more resistant to erosion and, thus, tended to form high peaks. Less resistant rocks, such as the younger, softer sedimentary rocks, were carved out as valleys and basins like North, Middle, and South Parks. Because the Laramide uplifts determined the distribution of resistant rocks, many of the present ranges mimic these older uplifts.

THREE

The Ice Ages

"And now there came both mist and snow,
And it grew wondrous cold. . . ."
SAMUEL TAYLOR COLERIDGE
"Rime of the Ancient Mariner", 1798

During much of the post-Laramide uplift, the climate in the Colorado mountains was generally temperate to tropical and the landscape was largely shaped by chemical decay of rocks and erosion by water. However, about 2.5 million years ago the climate began to alternate from warm to very cool and wet, and huge ice sheets spread across much of the northern part of North America. From the study of cores from the sea floor, we know that at least eight major glaciations have taken place in the last 800,000 years; however, evidence of all but the last few has been removed, concealed, or obliterated on land. No doubt some of these earlier glaciations played a role in shaping the Colorado mountains, but it is primarily the last two that have left conspicuous evidence of their presence.

The action of these glaciers in shaping the modern landscape is obvious to even the most casual mountain traveler. The ice-polished and striated rock surfaces, the U-shaped valleys, the scattered large boulders carried by the ice and marooned as it melted, and the glacial moraines—these all speak of the work of glaciers putting the final touches on the present mountain landscape. Although no great continental ice sheets edged into Colorado during the last half million years, careful mapping of glacial features suggests that all of the major Colorado ranges were festooned with glaciers or icefields during at least two recent glaciations, one between about 170,000 and 120,000 years ago, and one between 30,000 and 12,000 years ago. It was during the latter glaciation that the first humans appeared on the scene. During each of these glaciations, ice tongues extended down all the major mountain valleys, carving the cirques, polishing the valley walls, and scouring out basins for mountain lakes. In most of the larger valleys the farthest advance of the ice is marked by terminal moraines (U-shaped ridges of glacial debris, many of which pond scenic lakes) generally at elevations between 8,000 and 9,000 feet. Snow lines during these episodes may have been more than 3,000 feet lower and temperatures 20°F cooler. The last of the great mountain glaciers in Colorado began their final retreat about 12,000 years ago as the climate became warmer and dryer, reaching a "climatic optimum" between about 9,000 to 5,000 years ago. This period is called the "climatic optimum" because the average global temperature was slightly warmer than today's average global temperature, which implies a favorable climate, at least in regard to human needs.

A Primer on Glaciers

Glaciers form wherever more snow accumulates during the winter than is melted during the summer. As the snow piles deeper the buried layers are compressed and recrystallized to form ice, which then begins to flow under its own weight. Rocks that have fallen from the surrounding ridges or have been picked up from the underlying bedrock are incorporated in the moving ice mass and carried along. Ice in some of the large glaciers in Alaska moves hundreds or even thousands of feet per year, and transports huge volumes of rock debris. In fact, glaciers are far more effective agents of erosion than streams—this is why they have played such an important role in shaping the mountain landscape.

The rock-walled amphitheater at the head of a glaciated valley is called a cirque. The steep cirque walls develop as rocks are quarried by ice from the glacier bed or tumble onto the glacier from the valley walls. Commonly the glacier scoops out a shallow basin in the floor of the cirque. Many of the exquisite alpine lakes for which the Colorado mountains are famous are cradled in these cirque basins. The jagged peaks and saw-toothed ridges so characteristic of many of the ranges were sharpened by glacial erosion at the heads of the cirques that flank them.

As a glacier moves down a valley, it scours the valley bottom and walls. The efficiency of ice in this process is greatly increased by the presence of rock fragments in the ice which act as abrasives, much like the sand in sandpaper. The valley bottom is scraped, plowed, quarried, and swept clean of soil and loose rocks. Fragments of many sizes and shapes are dragged along the bottom of the moving ice and the hard ones scratch long parallel grooves in the underlying tough bedrock. Such grooves (glacial striae) record the direction of ice movement.

In the upper reaches of the glacier more ice accumulates in the winter than melts in the summer. At lower elevations farther down-valley, the glacier passes into a zone where more ice melts in the summer than is supplied by flow from above. This is the ablation zone. The line between the accumulation and ablation zones is called the equilibrium altitude. The position of the lower end of the glacier (the snout, or terminus) marks the place where the amount of ice supplied by flow from the upper reaches of the glacier exactly balances the amount that melts. We often speak of a glacier advancing or retreating, but it is important to remember that the ice is always moving down-valley. The advance or retreat of the terminus is determined by the delicate balance between rate of ice flow and rate of melting. Thus the position of the terminus is a very sensitive indicator of climate change.

Material carried down-glacier by the moving ice is released as the ice melts at the terminus. The semicircular ridge of glacial debris that marks the down-valley margin of the glacier is called a terminal (or end) moraine; a similarly formed ridge along the side of a glacier is a lateral moraine. Many valleys have a series of end moraines, each of which marks a place where the ice front remained stationary for a length of time. End moraines are generally formed by the slow accumulation of material in the same manner as that at the end of a conveyor belt; only rarely are they built by material pushed up ahead of the ice as if by a bulldozer. In many places end moraines act as natural dams that form scenic lakes in the valley bottoms. The material that forms the moraines is a mixture of rock fragments carried in the ice and the gravel, sand, and clay carried by streams flowing on or under the ice. Large boulders, some weighing hundreds of tons, carried by the ice are called erratics; many of these are scattered on the valley floors and on the flanks of the surrounding mountains.

Great volumes of water pour from melting ice near the lower end of a glacier. These streams, heavily laden with rock flour produced by the grinding action of the glacier and with rock debris liberated from the melting ice, erode gaps in the end moraine and spread a broad apron of sand and gravel down-valley from the glacier. Material deposited by streams issuing from a glacier is called outwash; the sheet of outwash in front of the glacier is called an outwash plain, or outwash fan if it is conical. If the glacier terminus is retreating, masses of old stagnant ice commonly are buried beneath the outwash; when these melt, the spaces they once occupied become deep round depressions called kettles; many of these now contain ponds or swamps.

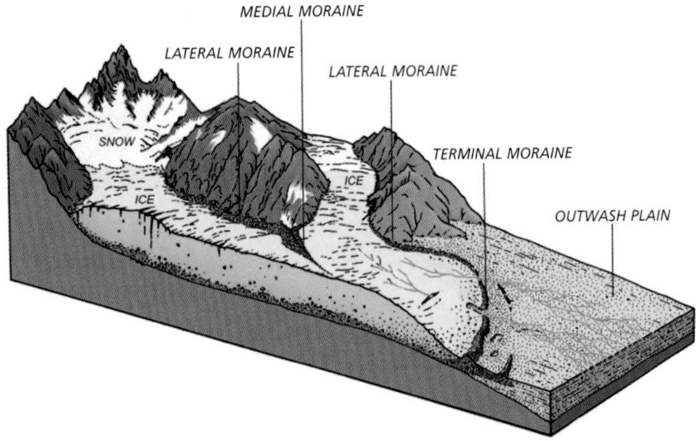

Cutaway drawing of a typical valley glacier. In the drawing the accumulation zone is shown as snow-covered; the ablation zone is shown as bare ice. This is the way the glacier would appear at the end of the melt season. Brown represents debris on, in, or under the ice. Yellow represents outwash. Note the old terminal moraine partly buried by outwash that marks an earlier position of the terminus. Reproduced by permission of the Grand Teton Natural History Association.

U-shaped valley of Maroon Creek in the Elk Mountains. Crater Lake (foreground) formed when a landslide from Pyramid Peak blocked the valley.

Glacial polish and striae on a bedrock outcrop. ULLI LIMPITLAW PHOTO

Although Colorado presently has no large glaciers, it does have a few small glaciers and perennial snow fields that aspire to glacier-hood. These are not remnants of the older, larger glaciers. Most of them formed during several cold intervals after the "climatic optimum", the latest of which was the so called "Little Ice Age", an interval of cold, moist climate between about 1300 and 1850 A.D.

Erratic boulders in till. RUSS ALLEN PHOTO

Not all of the alpine parts of the Colorado mountains were covered by glaciers during the Ice Ages. Some sizable tracts of the old post-Laramide land surface were preserved between the glaciated valleys. As you've trudged across these open areas of alpine tundra, you'll probably have noticed that this type of surface is highly variable. In some places the ground is relatively smooth and covered by short grasses and forbs. In other places there are vast fields of angular pieces of rock. Most curious of all are the places where the broken rocks are arranged not randomly but rather in long stripes or even in polygonal rings. What can possibly have happened to produce such strange configurations?

The smooth grassy areas probably represent parts of the old land surface where chemical weathering before and between the glaciations has decomposed the rocks to produce at least a thin mantle of soil. The extensive flat fields of shattered rock, often referred to as *felsenmeer* (German for "rock sea"), are the products of wedging apart and splintering of the rocks by

The Arapaho Glacier in the Front Range, one of the few existing glaciers in Colorado. The exposed ice is full of rock debris, which makes it appear gray in the photograph. Notice that annual layers are visible in the exposed gray ice. The layers formed where dust accumulated on the surface of the old snow is buried by new snow before the snow is converted to glacier ice. The milky turquoise color of the lake is due to rock flour (rock that has been pulverized into silt produced by the grinding action of the glacier) or by dust in the melting ice, and carried by melt water. RUSS ALLEN PHOTO

alternate freezing and thawing of water in joints and fractures. The upper slopes of many of the Colorado Fourteeners are covered with such rock fields—the Boulder Field on Longs Peak is one example.

Some slopes in the alpine tundra are decorated with curious arrangements of stones. Although you might expect stones of various sizes to be arranged more or less randomly, in some places you will find definite rings or polygons of stones. You can also see long stripes of stones that extend downslope for hundreds of feet. The polygons or stripes commonly contain nothing but stones, with little apparent soil between the blocks. Outside of the polygons or between the stripes there is much soil and vegetation

Non-glaciated upland surface near Hallett Peak in the Front Range
ULLI LIMPITLAW PHOTO

with scattered stones. It is as if the stones have been sorted and rearranged by some agent of nature, and indeed that is exactly what has happened. These rings, polygons, and stripes are collectively referred to as patterned ground. Patterned ground is widespread in arctic regions and is characteristic of areas of permanently frozen ground (permafrost). In fact, permafrost has been encountered in mine workings in several places in the Colorado mountains, and must have existed in much of the alpine zone during the Ice Ages.

How can rocks be selectively sorted into the features of patterned ground? The answer lies in the phenomenon of frost heave or the freeze-thaw cycle. Let's assume that the ground originally contained a relatively homogeneous mix of soil and larger

Patterned ground near Trinchera Peak in the Culebra Range. Red flags are survey markers placed by Prof. J. S. Alber of Emporia State University (Kansas) as part of a detailed study of how patterned ground forms. JAMES ALBER PHOTO

stones of various sizes. During warm weather the soil within a few inches or feet of the surface becomes saturated with water; when temperatures fall the water freezes. This freeze-thaw cycle can be repeated many times during the year, particularly if the ground beneath the surface layer is permanently frozen. Because water expands about ten percent when it freezes, the water-saturated soil expands pushing the stones upward. During the next thaw, fine soil material tends to ooze beneath the stones. Gradually, over many freeze-thaw cycles, the stones are brought to the surface. Once on the surface the stones tend to get pushed together because the areas of finer grained materials absorb more water and consequently expand more than the areas with more stones. Basically, the finer grained areas bulge up due to greater expansion, and the stones move downhill into the lower areas that underwent less expansion.

If the ground surface is nearly level, the stones are eventually arranged into rings or polygons; this is commonly the case on tops of rounded ridges and on some of the vast flat areas of alpine tundra. If the slope of the ground is steeper, however, then the arrangements of stones are elongated into distorted polygons or even into stripes. This distortion is caused by gravity which affects the dispersal of stones as they are subjected to the repeated cycles of freezing and thawing. On some of the rounded ridges along Trail Ridge Road in Rocky Mountain National Park, you can see both types of arrangements: stone rings occur on the tops of the ridges, and as you walk down the increasingly steeper sides you find rings distorted first into elongated polygons and then into long, discrete stone stripes.

AFTER THE ICE AGES

Most climbers are all too familiar with talus, the polite name for the broken rock that piles up below high cliffs. As water from rain or melting snow trickles into joints and fractures in the cliff face and then freezes and expands, the cracks are widened. As this never-ending freeze-thaw cycle continues season after season and year after year, even the most durable rocks are split and pieces are wedged off and tumble to the base of the cliff. Usually the pieces don't roll very far; instead they tend to pile up at the cliff base forming cones or aprons of angular blocks of rock.

Many of the most impressive piles of talus probably formed during the harsher climates that prevailed during and soon after the last retreat of the Ice Age glaciers. However, much talus is still forming today, as many climbers and hikers who have had close brushes with falling blocks can attest. If the rate of talus formation slows or even ceases, the pile of blocks stabilizes and the rocks are gradually covered by moss, lichens, and other vegetation. This provides a valuable route-finding tool to the mountain traveler: light-colored talus generally lacks vegetation and is probably unstable and difficult to walk over; darker-colored talus indicates vegetation is beginning to take hold and that the talus might be relatively stable and might provide easier walking. A special exception to this rule is that slopes of very small rock fragments, called scree, can provide welcome descent routes where you can shuffle, plunge-step, or even glissade effortlessly—but carefully!

In some places you will see irregular ridges of talus that lie along the lower edges of the talus fans and aprons below the base of a cliff. Although these talus ridges may resemble moraines deposited by a glacier, this is not the case. They are formed where rocks falling off the cliff face drop onto a snow bank and slide down to accumulate at the lower edge of the snow. When the snow bank melts the accumulated rocks form a ridge near the toe of the talus that is called a protalus rampart. A wonderful bit of trivia with which to impress your flatland friends!

In many of the Colorado ranges, cirques and glacial valleys contain tongue-shaped accumulations of talus with bulbous fronts at the lower end. In shape, these accumulations resemble glaciers and, indeed, they are called rock glaciers. In many cases, they look like an ice glacier from which the ice has been removed, leaving only the many stones it once carried. Measurement of the positions of markers placed on the surface of several Colorado rock glaciers show that they are moving, generally at rates of a few inches a year. If you were to dig into a rock glacier (not recommended), you might find there is still some residual ice between the blocks of rock, enough ice to allow the rock glacier to flow like a regular glacier, although much more slowly. These rock glaciers may be remnants of small glaciers formed during one of the several mini-glaciations that took place after the "climatic optimum" 9,000 years ago, but the ice in them may be partly sustained by freezing of rain and meltwater that trickle through their rock blankets to freeze at depth. Marvelous examples of rock glaciers can be found in the San Juan Mountains, the Elk Mountains, and the northern Front Range. We invite you to sit on a high ridge overlooking a rock glacier in the valley below and ponder the how and why of these intriguing alpine landforms. You might also want to ponder the best way to get around them, since they are generally very unstable and make for very difficult walking, as any one who has trekked across the one that guards the northeast ridge of North Maroon Peak can attest.

Even today erosion continues to shape the landscape. Rocks slowly decay and crumble under the attack of rain and organic acids. They are split and broken by freezing and thawing or wedged apart by roots. Although not as effective as glaciers in carving the landscape, avalanches, rock falls, mudflows, and

Small rock glacier near Torreys Peak in the Front Range. Bench at head of the rock glacier is a "protalus rampart". Note the other larger rock glaciers that project down into the timber on the slopes in the distance. ULLI LIMPITLAW PHOTO

landslides move soil and rocks down the mountain flanks, and flash floods sweep them downstream, cutting canyons and ultimately, after many stops along the way, depositing them in the Gulf of Mexico or the Gulf of California. It is estimated that the major canyons are being downcut at average rates of fractions of an inch per century; thus the canyons may be an inch or so deeper today than when George Washington was born.

Mankind helps the process along with road building, mining, timber cutting, and farming, but nature would have her way even without our help. There is no reason to believe that our present mountains are any more permanent than the Ancestral Rocky Mountains or the Laramide Rocky Mountains. The everlasting hills are a myth. The story we read in the rocks tells us that the modern landscape is merely one brief scene in an endless movie, the beginning of which we missed, and the end of which we will not live to see. Perhaps that is why we are so fascinated with mountains.

Are the Mountains Getting Higher?

This is a question that is often asked and to which we have no definitive answer. Current surveys are not precise enough to detect a change over a single lifetime, but it is possible that new surveys using Global Positioning System (GPS) technology might some day answer the question once and for all.

However, while we wait for the results from new GPS research, we can speculate. As we have seen, the land surface that developed after destruction of the Laramide mountains has apparently been uplifted a mile or more over the past 5 million years or so. This would amount to an average rate of uplift of about 1½ inches per century. There is no reason to believe that this regional uplift has stopped, but we have no way of knowing how fast it may be continuing. However, paleoseismologists, or geologists who study evidence of prehistoric earthquakes in the landscape, are gaining more understanding of how rapidly our landscape is uplifting, one earthquake at a time.

Even if the regional uplift has stopped, it is still likely that the peaks may in fact be getting higher. How can that be? The crust of the Earth is not rigid. It acts as a flexible sheet floating on fluid material in the Earth's mantle (the layer beneath the crust). You might picture it as resembling the upper surface of a water bed. If you put a weight (like a mountain) on it, it sinks down just as the surface of a water bed is depressed when you lie down on it. If you remove the weight, it pops back up.

So what happens when you erode a mountain? Imagine if you will, a barge loaded with a large rounded pile of sand, the top of which lies a certain distance above the level of the water on which the barge floats. Now suppose that you begin to shovel sand overboard from around the edges of the pile. As you remove sand the barge will rise higher in the water, and the top of the pile will go up. As you continue to remove sand, the top of the pile will continue to rise higher and higher. Only when you reach a point where the top of the pile begins to collapse will the elevation of the top above the water begin to decrease. In much the same way, removal of material from mountain valleys and slopes can cause the peaks of a mountain range to rise until erosion proceeds far enough to begin to collapse the summits.

Another way to remove weight from a mountain range is to melt glaciers and snowfields. Roughly 8,000 square miles in the Colorado mountains were covered with ice during the latest major episode of glaciation. Assuming the ice averaged about a quarter of a mile thick, about 900 million tons of ice were removed when these glaciers melted. We know that areas around the Baltic Sea, Hudson Bay, and parts of Alaska are still rising at rates of an inch or so a year. The glaciers in Colorado were much smaller than the glaciers were in those areas, but nevertheless it seems likely that post-glacial rebound is still a factor that probably contributes to continuing uplift of the Colorado mountains.

FOUR

Mountains Beyond Mountains

Describing and Comparing the Ranges of Colorado

"Snowy ranges, one behind another, extended to the distant horizon . . . with a single sweep, the eye takes in a distance of three hundred miles—that distance to the west, north, and south being made up of mountains ten, eleven, twelve, and thirteen thousand feet high . . . and between us and them lay glories of mountain, canyon, and lake, sleeping in depths of blue and purple most ravishing to the eye."

ISABELLA BIRD
"A Lady's Life in the Rocky Mountains", 1873

We have seen that the complex tapestry of the Colorado mountains is made up of a wide variety of rocks of different ages and types, formed over an immense span of geologic time, arranged and rearranged during at least three episodes of uplift, and sculpted for millennia by water, wind, and glacial ice. We have deciphered the outline of this story from the evidence contained in the rocks of the mountains, the deposits in the intervening basins

Satellite image of the Colorado mountains.

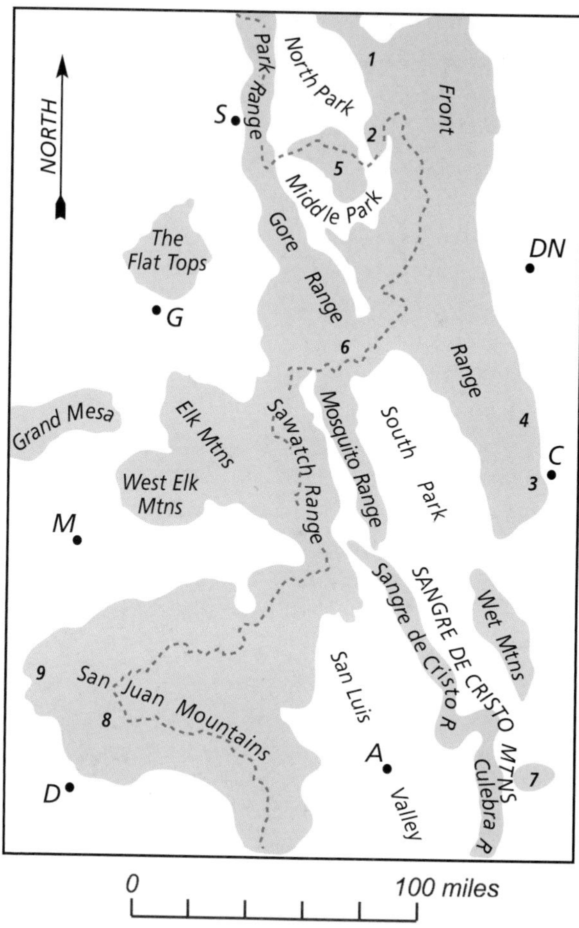

Names of mountain ranges and other geographic features. Cities: DN, Denver; C, Colorado Springs; A, Alamosa; D, Durango; M, Montrose; G, Glenwood Springs; S, Steamboat Springs. Small ranges: 1, Medicine Bow Mountains; 2, Never Summer Mountains; 3, Pikes Peak massif; 4, Rampart Range; 5, Rabbit Ears Range; 6, Tenmile Range; 7, Spanish Peaks; 8, Needle Mountains; 9, San Miguel Mountains. Dotted red line is the Continental Divide.

and surrounding plains, but the outline will continue to be revised and corrected and the details filled in for as long as geologists roam the hills.

Each of the Colorado Ranges contains clues to different parts of the geologic story, and these differences in geology account for many of the differences in aspect that the various ranges present to the mountain traveler—the colors of their rocks, the ruggedness of their slopes, the firmness of their footholds, the instability of their talus slopes, and the many other features that quicken the step or agitate the mind of the approaching climber. Thus, it is appropriate in the following sections that we explore the geology of each of the major ranges in somewhat greater detail. We will begin in the northeast with the Front Range and work our way west and south to the San Juan Mountains.

Geologic Maps

A geologic map shows the distribution of various kinds and ages of rocks and their relations to one another; it is an essential tool of the geologist's trade. Most geologists spend their careers making geologic maps, and interpreting, refining, or generalizing other people's geologic maps. Such maps are essential in unraveling the geologic history of a region, whether it be a continent, a country, a mountain range, or your own backyard. We have therefore included geologic maps of each of the major mountain ranges discussed in this section of the book, with the exception of the Culebra Range and the Spanish Peaks. Each of the geologic maps is accompanied by an explanation of the colors, patterns, and symbols it employs, and by a LANDSAT satellite image of the same area with peaks, roads, towns, streams, and other geographic features labeled. The same roads, streams, and symbols for peaks and towns are repeated on the geologic maps, but to avoid clutter they are not labeled. Peaks are shown by small white triangles bordered by red lines for Fourteeners and by black lines for other peaks mentioned in the text.

The geologic maps are largely based on the 1:500,000-scale geologic map of Colorado published by the U.S. Geological Survey in 1976, but newer information has been added to several of the maps. The maps are at various scales, depending on the size of the area and on the amount of detail they portray. They have been greatly simplified, and the rock units grouped on the basis of the parts of the geologic story to which they pertain. The geologic maps have been overlaid on a shaded-relief model prepared from satellite data with 30-meter resolution.

We have avoided using traditional geologic map colors and patterns and have chosen instead to use colors and patterns that emphasize rock units of greatest interest to mountaineers. The colors and patterns for each rock unit are shown in boxes in the explanation for each map. Because of the shading on the relief model, colors have a somewhat different appearance on heavily shaded areas than on areas of lighter shading—to try to overcome this, we have placed color and pattern swatches in the explanation over a piece of a relief model with a typical range of shading. In the center of each rock unit box on the explanations there is a letter symbol. The same letter symbols are strategically placed on the map to help the reader identify the map units. The unit labels are in black type in lightly shaded parts of the map and in white type in more heavily shaded areas.

FRONT RANGE

The Front Range forms the eastern rampart of the Rocky Mountains in central and northern Colorado. It is a large range—about one hundred and fifty miles long and forty miles wide—that encompasses all the complex array of ranges and uplands that lie west of the Great Plains and east of North Park,

Middle Park, and South Park. It includes a number of geographically and geologically distinct subranges, including the Mummy Range, the Never Summer Mountains, the Tarryall Mountains, the Rampart Range, and the Pikes Peak massif. The uplands extend northward into the Laramie Range and northwestward into the Medicine Bow Mountains, both of which lie mainly in Wyoming. On the south, the Front Range is bounded by the Arkansas River. The Continental Divide follows the crest of the range southward from the northern end of the Never Summer Mountains to the vicinity of Argentine Pass. The only two 14,000-foot peaks in all of Colorado that actually lie on the divide are Grays Peak and Torreys Peak, which are in this range.

The Front Range is carved principally in basement rocks—ancient metamorphic and igneous rocks that form the underpinnings of this part of the North American continent. The metamorphic rocks are largely mica gneiss and schist formed by metamorphism of sedimentary rocks, and felsic gneiss and amphibolite, formed by the metamorphism of volcanic rocks. The metamorphic rocks are all about 1.8 to 1.7 billion years old. The igneous rocks are mostly granite that invaded the metamorphic rocks during three different episodes, the first about 1.7 billion years, ago, the second about 1.4 billion years ago, and the third about 1.0 billion years ago.

Uplift of the basement rocks that form the core of the present Front Range began about 65 million years ago, during the early stages of the Laramide orogeny. Although details remain obscure, it appears that a slab of basement rocks and their sedimentary

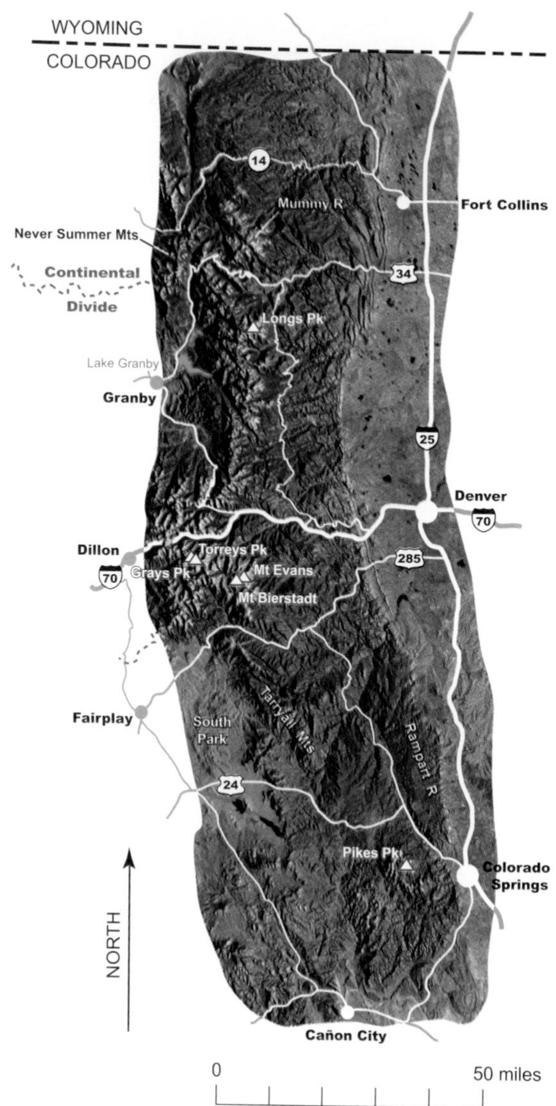

Satellite image of the Front Range showing geographic features.

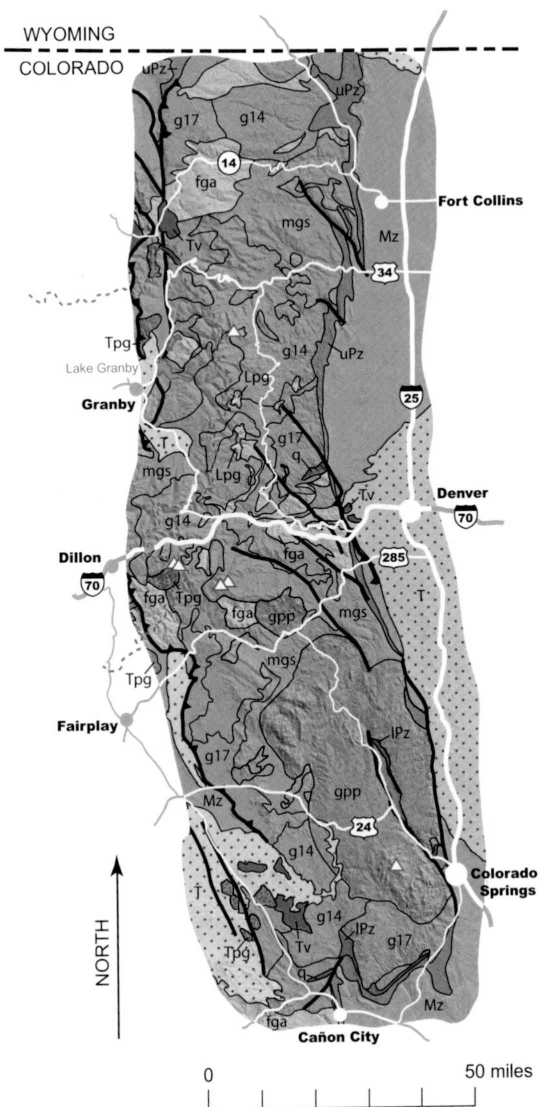

Geologic map of the Front Range.

EXPLANATION

Tertiary volcanic rocks

Tertiary porphyry and granite (intruded after the Laramide orogeny)

Tertiary sedimentary rocks

Porphyry and granite (intruded during the Laramide orogeny)

Mesozoic sedimentary rocks (mostly deposited in or near the great Cretaceous seaway)

Upper Paleozoic sedimentary rocks (mostly deposited during uplift and erosion of the Ancestral Rocky Mountains)

Lower Paleozoic sedimentary rocks (deposited in shallow seas)

Basement Rocks

Pikes Peak granite (intruded about 1.0 billion years ago)

Quartzite

Granite (intruded about 1.4 billion years ago)

Mica gneiss, schist, and migmatite

Felsic gneiss and amphibolite

Granite (intruded about 1.7 billion years ago)

Symbols

Geologic contact

High- angle fault

Thrust fault (teeth on upper plate)

Explanation for geologic map of the Front Range.

cover were carried eastward over similar rocks that underlie the high plains. The eastern margin of the range is marked by a series of folds and faults along which basement rocks of the range were raised as much as four miles above the same basement rocks to the east. The blanket of sedimentary rocks above the basement was broken and tilted along the edge of the uplift forming the Flatirons near Boulder, Dinosaur Ridge and Red Rocks near Denver, and Garden of the Gods near Colorado Springs. Eventually the eastward-moving slab encountered so much resistance that it fractured along what is now the west side of the range, and sedimentary rocks to the west were shoved as much as six to eight miles eastward beneath the basement rocks of the Front Range.

During and after the Laramide orogeny, the basement rocks and their cover of younger sedimentary rocks were intruded by numerous large and small bodies of light-colored granite and porphyry. Most of the granite and porphyry intrusions lie in a narrow northeast-to-southwest-trending belt that extends across the Front Range from near Keystone to the mountains north of Boulder. These igneous intrusions mark part of the Colorado Mineral Belt, which in the Front Range includes the mining districts around Montezuma, Silver Plume, Georgetown, Idaho Springs, Gold Hill, and Boulder.

Remnants of the post-Laramide erosion surface are widespread in the eastern parts of the Front Range, especially in the foothills west and southwest of Denver, where the old land surface is preserved on the level crests of flat-topped ridges. Much of the site of the present Front Range was covered by volcanic rocks resembling those in the San Juan Mountains, but these have been almost entirely stripped away by erosion, leaving only a few small remnants around Specimen Mountain in Rocky Mountain National Park.

The northern and central parts of the Front Range are highly asymmetric. In this segment of the range all the high peaks lie in a narrow belt along the western side of the range. Most of the rest of these parts of the Front Range are a rugged forested upland with only a few peaks that approach timberline. A glance at the geologic map shows that the curious arrangement of high peaks is quite independent of the distribution of the various rock types. The asymmetry may be due to uplift of basement rocks along the western side of the range as rocks from the west were shoved beneath them during the Laramide orogeny; it may also be due in part to later uplift of the western edge of the range by younger faulting related to the opening of the Rio Grande rift.

During the Ice Ages the belt of high peaks supported extensive glaciers that extended eastward down the major canyons, some for distances of ten to fifteen miles. Small glaciers flowed westward, leaving conspicuous moraines around Grand Lake and Winter Park. Except for several small isolated glaciers on Pikes Peak, there is no evidence for glaciation in the southern Front Range during the most recent Ice Ages. The largest glaciers on Pikes Peak were on its southern and southwestern flanks, probably because the peak is the easternmost high peak in the range and thus accumulated snow from upslope flow of moisture from storms originating in the Gulf of Mexico. However, smaller glaciers occupied spectacular cirques on the north and northeast sides of the mountain.

A dozen or so perennial snowfields lie nestled in shady cirques in the northern part of the Front Range. Several of these have been called "glaciers", but only a few have been shown to be actually moving, most notably the Arapaho Glacier in the cirque beneath North and South Arapaho Peaks. These small snowfields and glaciers are not remnants of the large Ice Age glaciers; they formed during the so-called "Little Ice Age" between 1300 and 1850 A.D. and are now rapidly wasting away.

Never Summer Mountains

The Never Summer Mountains are a small north-south-trending subsidiary of the Front Range that lies along the northwestern boundary of Rocky Mountain National Park, between Cascade Mountain and Cameron Pass. Its crest lies along the Continental Divide. The range is largely composed of basement rocks, chiefly dark mica gneiss and schist similar to that which is widely exposed among the basement rocks in other parts of the Front Range. The basement rocks in the Never Summer Mountains are part of a thin wedge of basement rocks above one of the eastward-sloping faults that developed along the western edge of the Front Range during the Laramide orogeny. As mountain-building compression continued, sedimentary rocks that once lay west of the uplift were shoved several miles eastward down and under the basement wedge. Later, the basement wedge was severed from the main mass of the Front Range by a complicated zone of steeply inclined north-south-trending faults, part of the zone of faults that may have elevated the western edge of the main range.

The valley of the Colorado River has been carved by erosion in the broken rocks along this fault zone, which seems to have localized the intrusion of several large masses of granite and porphyry about 30 million years ago. Because these igneous bodies are more resistant to erosion, they form the high peaks along the range crest from Mt. Cirrus to Mt. Richthofen. As the bodies of magma that formed these igneous intrusions moved upward, they broke through the fault at the base of the basement wedge and carried with them some of the sedimentary rocks from beneath the wedge. The magma bodies apparently broke through to the surface to form volcanoes that were the source for the volcanic rocks around Specimen Mountain east of the fault zone.

Mummy Range

The Mummy Range is a small group of prominent peaks that form a north-trending spur of the Front Range from Fall River north to the northern boundary of Rocky Mountain National Park. The peaks are all in basement rocks of the Front Range uplift. The southern peaks—Mt. Chapin, Mt. Chiquita, and Ypsilon Mountain—are carved largely in dark mica gneiss and schist like that in the Never Summer Range. The northern peaks—Fairchild Mountain, Hagues Peak, Mummy Mountain, and Howe Mountain—are mostly in coarse-grained 1.4-billion-year-old granite, although several bodies of dark coarse-grained igneous rock called gabbro are prominent on the ridges of Howe Mountain. Many of the smooth slopes and flat-topped ridges are probably remnants of the post-Laramide erosion surface.

Central Front Range

From the Mummy Range south to the Tarryall Mountains, the Front Range consists almost entirely of basement rocks, chiefly dark mica gneiss and schist, layered felsic gneiss and amphibolite, and granite, locally intruded by granite and porphyry that were emplaced during and after the Laramide orogeny. Some of the principal Laramide intrusive bodies are around Mt. Audubon, near Eldora, at Empire, and around Montezuma.

Talus and felsenmeer on the Boulder Field on Longs Peak. All the rocks in the picture are 1.4 billion-year-old granite of the Longs Peak–St. Vrain batholith, except for a few dark slabs of wall rocks (chiefly biotite gneiss) exposed on the face near the right side of the photo.

Longs Peak and its neighbors are largely carved in coarse-grained granite that is about 1.4 billion years old. The granite is coarse grained and light colored and contains large slabs and irregular bodies of dark mica schist that were ripped off the walls of the

East face of South Arapaho Peak. Dark biotite gneiss and schist laced with dikes of 1.4-billion-year-old granite and pegmatite. Face is about 250 feet high. BRUCE BRYANT PHOTO

magma chamber as the granite was emplaced. From the Indian Peaks south to Guanella Pass the crest of the range is largely underlain by dark mica gneiss and schist and irregular bodies of both 1.4- and 1.7-billion-year-old granite, locally intensely fractured by Laramide and post-Laramide faults. Grays Peak and Torreys Peak are both largely mica gneiss and schist, laced with many dikes of pegmatite. A sizable body of light-colored granite, emplaced after the Laramide orogeny, forms the Montezuma stock just to the west of Grays and Torreys Peaks, and a small body of similar rocks forms the southwestern summit slopes of Torreys Peak. Dikes of light-colored porphyry injected at the same time as the young granite cut the gneiss and schist, especially on the northeastern ridge of Torreys (the Kelso Ridge). Mt. Evans, Mt. Bierstadt, and their neighboring peaks are all carved in a large body of streaky coarse-grained granite once thought to be 1.7 billion years old, but recently shown to be part of the group of 1.4-billion-year-old granites.

Tarryall Mountains

The Tarryall Mountains are a small group of ridges and peaks in the Front Range that lie along the east side of South Park, southeast of Kenosha Pass. The northwestern part of the Tarryalls is underlain with mica gneiss and schist like that farther north in the central Front Range. The southeastern part is coarse-grained granite that is part of the approximately one-billion-year-old granite body that forms Pikes Peak and the Rampart Range discussed below.

Pikes Peak Massif and the Rampart Range

Much of the southern part of the Front Range is carved in an enormous body of granite called the Pikes Peak batholith. The batholith was emplaced about one billion years ago and thus is the youngest of all the granite bodies among the basement rocks in the Front Range. It is unique in that it is the youngest granite known among the basement rocks in Colorado; the nearest exposures of granite of this age are in the Adirondack Mountains and in eastern Canada. The granite is mostly a very uniform, pink-to-orange rock that forms huge rounded boulders, spectacular spires, and gigantic smooth slabs, which produce unusual scenic topography in the Pikes Peak massif, the Rampart Range, the eastern Tarryall Range, and Lost Creek Wilderness. The summit of Pikes Peak itself is in a small irregular body of finer-grained light-colored granite that intrudes the Pikes Peak batholith, but which is of the same general age.

A conspicuous feature of the Rampart Range is the flat, even surfaces of most of the ridges. These flat ridge-tops are apparently remnants of the old post-Laramide landscape into which the streams carved their valleys during rapid uplift of the region during the past 5 million years. The flat surface was apparently particularly well developed in this area because the Pikes Peak granite was easily decomposed during the 30-million-year intervals of weathering and erosion before the rapid uplift. During the uplift the surface was broken by faults. The old land surface on the Rampart Range was raised as much as 1,000 feet above the same surface to the west along the Ute Pass fault. The valley of Trout Creek, which separates the Rampart Range from the lower hills to the west, is carved along this fault. The high smooth shoulders on the north, west, and south flanks of Pikes Peak may also be remnants of the post-Laramide land surface raised along faults during the late uplift of the region.

THE "PARK RANGES"

"Starting out as the Sierra Madres in Wyoming, the Park Range on contemporary maps now assumes independent names and identities as it works its way south; Park Range in the northern-most section, then the Gore Range, Tenmile Range, and Mosquito Range, the southernmost. The original designation of the entire range by early surveyors, impressed by the massive mountain parks on its flank, is repeated here more as a matter of convenient categorization than anything else."

Guide to the Colorado Mountains, 9th edition

On one of the earliest detailed topographic maps of Colorado, published by the Hayden Survey in 1877, the narrow, slightly sinuous mountain chain that extends south-southeastward from the Sierra Madre in southern Wyoming to the Arkansas River east of Salida was collectively labeled the Park Range. These ranges, which in modern usage include the Park, Gore, Tenmile, and Mosquito Ranges, all represent the eroded roots of basement-cored uplifts that developed early in the Laramide orogeny, between about 70 and 65 million years ago. The differences in character among these closely related ranges depend partly on the types of basement rocks that form them, partly on how much they were uplifted during the Laramide orogeny, and partly on their history of uplift and erosion since the time of the Laramide orogeny.

Park Range

Strictly speaking, the name Park Range now applies to the group of mountains that forms the Continental Divide between the head of the Encampment River, about nine miles south of the Wyoming state line, and the point near Rabbit Ears Pass, where it turns eastward to the crest of the Front Range. Although the highest peaks in the range are only slightly above 12,000 feet, the spectacular alpine scenery of the Mount Zirkel Wilderness attracts serious hikers and backpackers seeking to avoid the throngs on the Fourteeners. The peaks and canyons in most of the Wilderness are carved in layered metamorphic rocks, chiefly felsic gneiss and amphibolite, interlayered and inter-fingered with streaky red to gray granite that dates from about 1.7 billion years ago, during the first episode of granite intrusion in the basement rocks of Colorado. Layering in the metamorphic rocks and streaky alignment of minerals in the granite are steeply inclined or vertical. Erosion of the steeply tilted hard and soft layers in these rocks produces the jagged ridges and peaks that characterize the area around Mt. Zirkel and its neighbors. The southern part of the Park Range is carved in a five-to-six-mile-wide body of 1.4-billion-year-old granite that extends across the range just north of Rabbit Ears Pass. This area of granite includes the southern part of the Mount Zirkel Wilderness around Mt. Ethel. In many places the granite contains rectangular crystals of potassium feldspar an inch or more long that stand out as projections on weathered surfaces, offering traction for boot soles and convenient toe- and fingerholds. In most areas the granite is sparsely jointed and forms prominent ledges, canyon walls, and cirque headwalls.

The southeastern edge of the large body of 1.4-billion-year-old granite is coincident with a broad northeast-trending zone of faults within which the metamorphic rocks and older granite have been crushed, flattened, and recrystallized by fault movements that carried rocks northwest of the zone as much as fifteen miles southwestward with respect to rocks southeast of the zone. Most of this movement took place during or after emplacement of the 1.4-billion-year-old granite and before deposition of Mesozoic rocks on the flanks of the range, but some of the faults may have been locally reactivated during the Laramide orogeny. This fault zone effectively marks the southern end of the alpine topography in the Park Range; south of the fault, the remainder of the range is a broad timbered plateau underlain largely by old granite and capped locally by patches of post-Laramide sand and gravel interlayered with flows of basalt, one of which has been eroded to form the twin spires that give Rabbit Ears Pass its name.

Although the peaks in the Park Range only reach modest elevations, the area above snow line during the Ice Ages was very large, and the range was at times mantled by an ice cap that fed valley glaciers, some of which extended down-valley five miles or more beyond the mountain front. Glacial ice

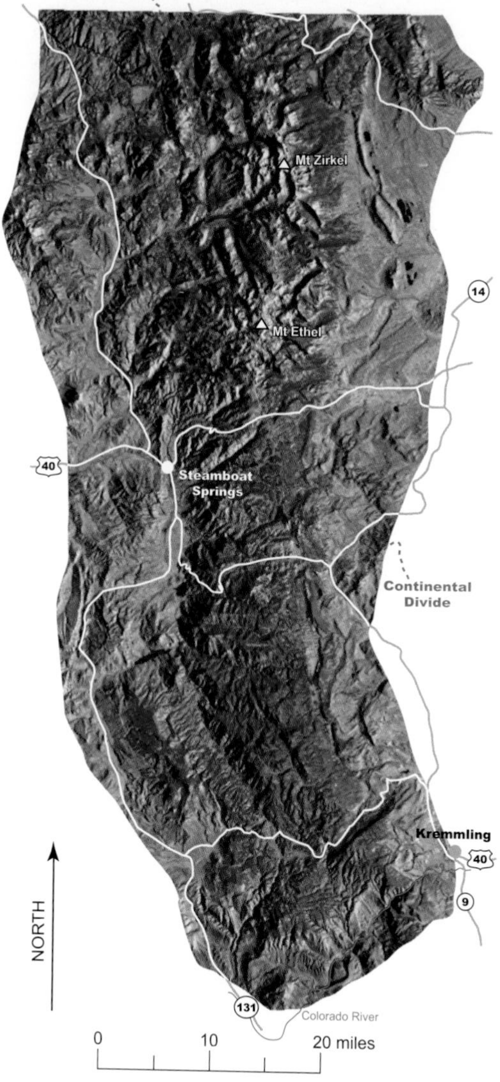

Satellite image of the Park and northern Gore Ranges showing geographic features.

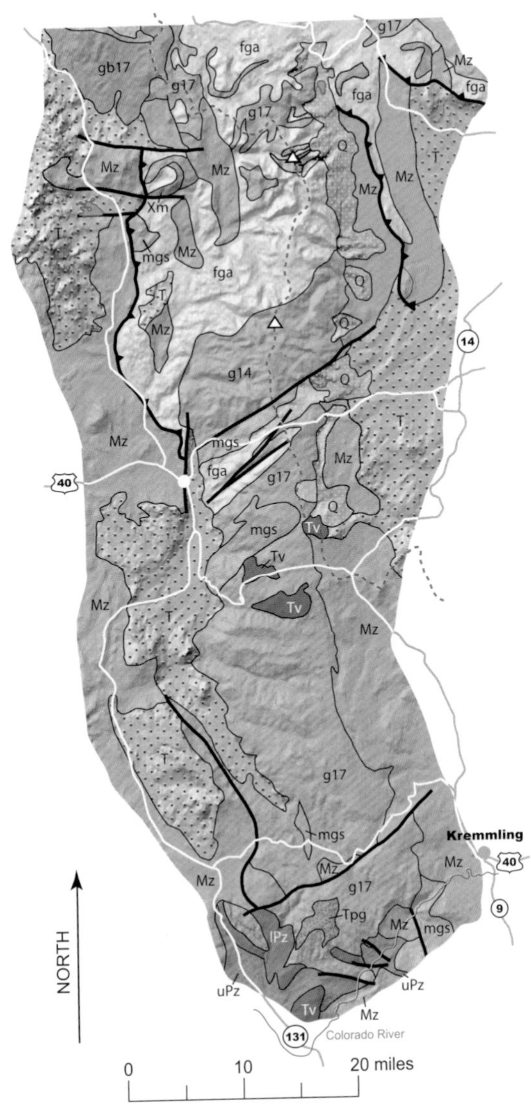

Geologic map of the Park and northern Gore Ranges.

EXPLANATION

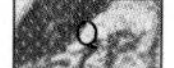

Quaternary deposits
(deposited by streams, glaciers, landslides, or other surficial processes)

Tertiary volcanic rocks

Tertiary porphyry and granite
(intruded after the Laramide orogeny)

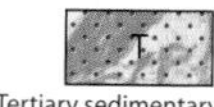

Tertiary sedimentary rocks

Mesozoic sedimentary rocks
(mostly deposited in or near the great Cretaceous seaway)

Upper Paleozoic sedimentary rocks
(mostly deposited during uplift and erosion of the Ancestral Rocky Mountains)

Lower Paleozoic sedimentary rocks
(deposited in shallow seas)

Basement Rocks

Granite
(intruded about 1.4 billion years ago)

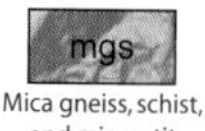

Mica gneiss, schist, and migmatite

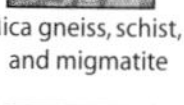

Felsic gneiss and amphibolite

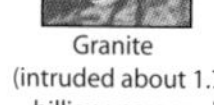

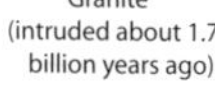

Granite
(intruded about 1.7 billion years ago)

Gabbro and related dark plutonic rocks
(intruded about 1.7 billion years ago)

Symbols

Geologic contact

High-angle fault

Thrust fault
(teeth on upper plate)

Explanation for geologic map of the Park and northern Gore Ranges.

sculpted the cirque basins, many of which are now filled with the lakes that dot the landscape in the higher parts of the range. The characteristic U-shaped valleys, the ice-polished rock faces, and the large terminal moraines at the canyon mouths all attest to the work of glaciers in shaping the landscape. In several places in the higher parts of the range the old post-Laramide land surface escaped destruction by glacial erosion and survives as high flat-topped ridges at elevations between 11,500 and 12,000 feet.

Northern Gore Range

The northern segment of the Gore Range between Rabbit Ears Pass and the Colorado River is a southward continuation of the plateau of the southern Park Range. The plateau is tilted gently westward, so that the drainage divide is along its eastern edge. The plateau surface is generally at elevations below 10,000 feet, but a few knobs have elevations of as much as 10,500 feet. The surface is deeply dissected by west-flowing streams. Although this part of the Gore Range is of little interest to climbers or hikers seeking alpine scenery, it is dearly beloved by cross-country skiers and snowshoers (not to mention snowmobilers). Except for the area immediately south of Rabbit Ears Pass, the plateau surface has not been glaciated. The difference between the alpine scenery of the Park Range and the more subdued topography of the northern Gore Range can be attributed in part to differences in the amount of uplift of the basement rocks during the Laramide orogeny and during subsequent faulting.

How did the Colorado River cut Gore Canyon, the spectacular V-shaped gorge that slices through the Gore Range below Kremmling? The answer is that the river established its westward course out of North Park during or shortly after the Laramide orogeny. At that time the river and its tributaries flowed across clay, sand, and gravel that filled the basin between the rising Laramide Front Range and Park Range uplifts and also covered the areas south and east of the Park Range. Faulting and uplift associated with opening of the Rio Grande rift, which began about 26 million years ago, accelerated erosion, causing the streams to cut rapidly downward into the soft basin-fill. Where a west-flowing stream encountered hard basement rocks beneath the blanket of soft basin fill deposits, it was diverted to join a nearby stream that had not yet cut down to the basement rocks.

Remains of one such abandoned channel are preserved as a narrow ridge of gravel that crosses the Gore Range about thirteen miles south of Rabbit Ears Pass. The "Trough Road" between Kremmling and Radium follows another abandoned channel just south of Gore Canyon. This process continued until ultimately all of the drainage from Middle Park was combined into the main stem of the Colorado River, which had sought out the place where the basement rocks lie at the lowest possible elevation. There it was forced to cut into the basement rocks, producing the magnificent 2,000-foot-deep slot that allows the Denver and Rio Grande Railroad access to the Western Slope and provides rafters and kayakers with world-class paddling.

Southern Gore Range

From Gore Canyon, the Gore Range continues southeastward as an unimpressive forested ridge cored by basement rocks (chiefly biotite gneiss and schist and granite). The flanks of the ridge are covered with soft Mesozoic sedimentary rocks, chiefly black shale, and locally these rocks extend all the way to the ridge crest, making wet-weather driving problematic. The ridge crest rises gradually southward and reaches timberline on Elliott Ridge about twelve miles southeast of the Gore Canyon. Suddenly, about twenty miles south of the canyon, the high alpine meadows of Elliott Ridge give way to the spectacular jagged peaks of Eagles Nest and Mt. Powell. Mt. Powell (13,560+ feet) the highest peak in the range, was one of the principal control stations used by the Hayden Survey when they mapped this part of Colorado in the 1870s. Although the alpine part of the Gore Range contains no 14,000-foot peaks, it boasts a dozen or more above 13,000 feet and many above 12,500 feet, and they are among the most rugged, spectacular, and challenging in Colorado. In the eighteen-mile segment of the range between Eagles Nest and I-70 in Tenmile Canyon, less than a dozen peaks have been officially named, although several bear informal names bestowed by climbers and guidebook authors. U.S. Geological Survey Bulletin 1319-C by Ogden Tweto, Bruce Bryant, and Frank Williams described the alpine part of the Gore Range as follows:

> "The high part of the Gore Range…consists of a sinuous knife-edge crestal spine and a series of

> attached high spur ridges separated by deep glaciated canyons. Many of the spur ridges are equally as high and jagged as the main crest, and in most views from the highways they form the skyline, hiding the main crest. All the high slopes and ridges are bare rock..., either in cliffs and outcroppings, or in fields of frost-riven boulders. The bottoms of the canyons between the ridges are glacially smoothed bedrock which in many places is covered by a dense spruce forest up to a timberline altitude of about 11,000 feet. The canyon walls are a succession of forbidding cliffs extending to the upper limit of glacial cutting, which in most places is near the ridge tops. At the base of the cliffs, and covering the lower sides of the valleys, are almost continuous blankets of debris consisting of talus, avalanche, rock-slide, and alluvial-cone deposits."

The high part of the Gore Range is carved from an uplifted block of basement rock that lies between the Gore fault on the southwest and the Frontal fault on the northeast. The Gore fault separates the basement rocks on the northeast from gently inclined late Paleozoic sedimentary rocks deposited during the uplift of the Ancestral Rocky Mountains on the southwest. Changes in thickness of some of these deposits across the fault suggest that it was active during this early period of uplift, but it was also active both during and after the Laramide orogeny. The fault is beautifully exposed along Booth Creek north of East Vail, where the sedimentary beds southwest of the fault are bent upward and locally overturned by the fault movement. On the other

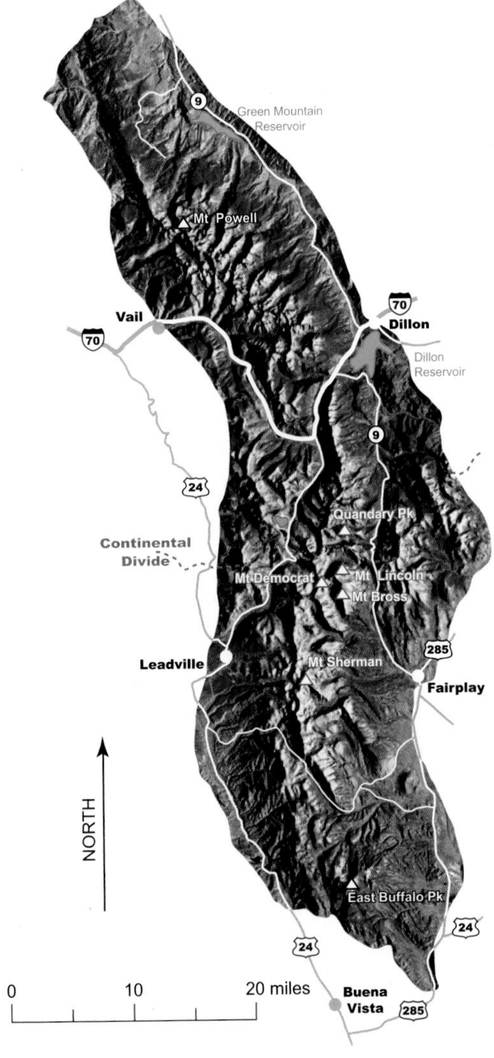

Satellite image of the southern Gore, Tenmile, and Mosquito Ranges showing geographic features.

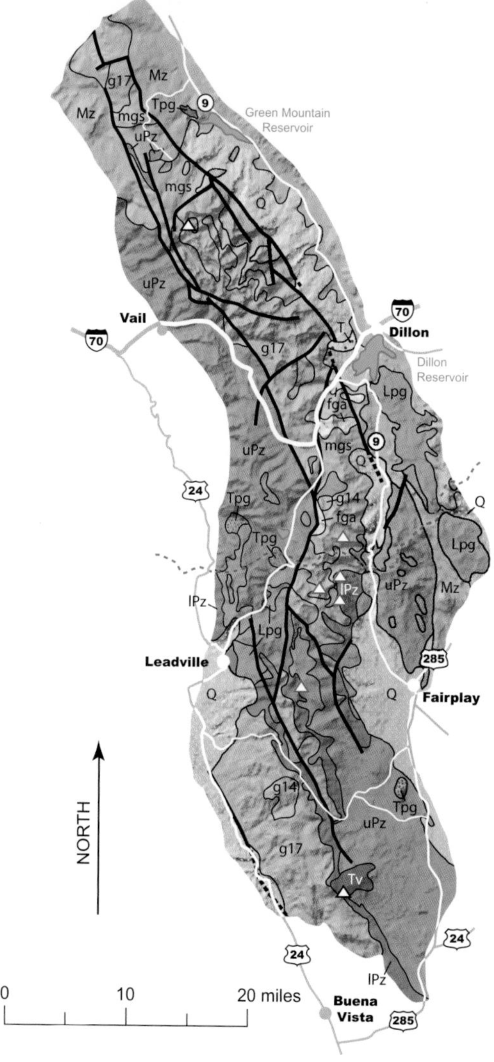

Geologic map of the southern Gore, Tenmile, and Mosquito Ranges.

EXPLANATION

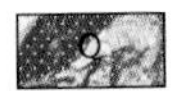

Quaternary deposits
(deposited by streams, glaciers, landslides, or other surficial processes)

Tertiary volcanic rocks

Tertiary porphyry and granite
(intruded after the Laramide orogeny)

Tertiary sedimentary rocks

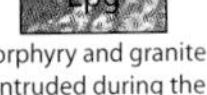

Porphyry and granite
(intruded during the Laramide orogeny)

Mesozoic sedimentary rocks
(mostly deposited in or near the great Cretaceous seaway)

Upper Paleozoic sedimentary rocks
(mostly deposited during uplift and erosion of the Ancestral Rocky Mountains)

Lower Paleozoic sedimentary rocks
(deposited in shallow seas)

Basement Rocks

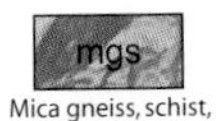

Mica gneiss, schist, and migmatite

Felsic gneiss and amphibolite

Granite
(intruded about 1.4 billion years ago)

Granite
(intruded about 1.7 billion years ago)

Symbols

Geologic contact

High-angle fault

Thrust fault
(teeth on upper plate)

Explanation for geologic map of the southern Gore, Tenmile, and Mosquito Ranges.

side of the range, the Frontal fault separates basement rocks of the Gore Range from Mesozoic black shale and white sandstone deposited in the Great Cretaceous Seaway. The Frontal fault is almost completely buried beneath glacial deposits, but fresh fault breaks in glacial moraines suggest that movement is still continuing along it. This suggests that the Frontal fault is part of a newly opening offshoot of the Rio Grande rift. Studies of radiation damage in certain mineral crystals confirm that much of the uplift of the alpine parts of the Gore Range took place in the last 10–20 million years, making it one of the youngest ranges in Colorado. Will Mt. Powell be our next Fourteener?

The basement rocks of the alpine part of the Gore Range are a complicated mixture of biotite gneiss and migmatite and 1.7-billion-year-old granite. Migmatitic biotite gneiss makes up most of the

Jagged peaks in granite and migmatitic gneiss along the crest of the southern Gore Range. Mount of the Holy Cross in the northern Sawatch Range is in the background. BRUCE BRYANT PHOTO

northern and southern parts of the high Gore Range; light- to medium-gray granite makes up most of the central part. The granite bodies interfinger with the migmatitic gneiss, and commonly contain layers, pods, or streaks of gneiss.

The layering in the gneiss and the mineral streaking in the granite are generally steeply or moderately inclined and highly variable in trend. The rocks are broken by a complex array of faults, many of which trend northwest-southeast, more or less parallel to the range, and others which trend more or less east-west. Closely spaced south-sloping joints are widespread in much of the range. Weathering and erosion along these joints and faults produces notches and couloirs in the ridges that greatly enhance the alpine character of these mountains. Glaciers have carved all of the major canyons and spread great loops of glacial till on the flanks of the range. At times glaciers on the northeast side of the range extended all the way down to the Blue River and may at times have blocked the river to produce short-lived, ice-dammed lakes.

One important geologic feature of the high Gore Range is the essentially complete absence of Laramide and post-Laramide granite and porphyry and thus the lack of mineral deposits associated with them in the nearby parts of the Colorado Mineral Belt. For this reason the range lacks the mine roads and railroad grades that provide easy access to many of the other ranges and the mine dumps, tailings ponds, and mill sites that scar their slopes and valleys.

Tenmile and Mosquito Ranges

The same uplifted rib of basement rocks that forms the Park and Gore Ranges continues southward to form the Tenmile and Mosquito Ranges. The boundary between the Gore Range and the Tenmile Range is arbitrarily placed at Tenmile Canyon, the canyon followed by I-70 between Frisco and Vail Pass. Just as arbitrarily, the line between the Tenmile and Mosquito Ranges is placed along the segment of the Continental Divide that crosses the mountains between Hoosier Pass and Fremont Pass. Thus, streams draining the Tenmile Range flow into the Blue River or Eagle River; those from the Mosquito Range drain into the Arkansas or the Platte.

Although not quite as spectacular, the topography of the Tenmile and northernmost parts of the Mosquito Range is similar to that of the alpine parts of

The crest of the Mosquito Range near Horseshoe Mountain. East-sloping layers of lower Paleozoic sedimentary rocks (red and brown) injected by sills of porphyry (light gray to white) rest on basement rocks (darker gray or brown) on the lower part of the ridge that slopes down to the left edge of the photo. Thick sills of porphyry underlie the smooth ridges in the right side of the photo. ULLI LIMPITLAW PHOTO

the Gore Range. The Tenmile Range contains only one Fourteener, Quandary Peak, but the rugged peaks, jagged ridges, glaciated valleys, and easy accessibility make the range a favorite of hikers and climbers. This rugged topography continues south into the Mosquito Range as far as the triad of Fourteeners comprising Mt. Bross, Mt. Lincoln, and Mt. Democrat. From there south, the scenery is less spectacular—the ridges are more rounded, the glaciated valleys wider, and the slopes are smoother. Only one Fourteener, Mt. Sherman, perhaps the easiest to climb in the state, lies in the southern Mosquito Range.

The west side of the Tenmile-Mosquito uplift is bounded by the Mosquito and Weston faults. The northeast-trending Mosquito fault separates basement rocks of the uplift on the east from late Paleozoic sedimentary rocks on the west. It intersects the northwest-trending Gore fault just south of Copper Mountain. The Weston fault is a northwest-trending fault that breaks through the basement rocks and drops the basement rocks southwest of the fault a thousand feet or more relative to the basement rock in the high ridges northeast of the fault. Both the Weston fault and the parallel London fault, about six miles to the northeast, were probably formed during the opening of the Rio Grande rift, which forms the upper Arkansas valley south of Leadville. The mountainous part of the Mosquito Range ends approximately at Weston Pass, southwest of Mt. Sherman, where the northwest-trending Weston fault cuts the range crest. From there the Mosquito Range dwindles to a belt of low but rugged ridges that extend southward to the Arkansas River near Salida.

The eastern frontal fault of the Gore Range dies out just south of the northern tip of the Tenmile Range. From there southward the basement rocks on the eastern flank of the uplift are overlain by gently east-sloping layers of early and late Paleozoic sedimentary rocks that disappear beneath younger deposits in South Park. Patches of these sedimentary rocks extend almost to the range crest and cap the summits of Quandary Peak, Mt. Lincoln, and Mt. Bross.

The basement rocks in the Tenmile and Mosquito Ranges are predominantly migmatitic biotite gneiss and schist similar to those in the southern Gore Range, but in the northern Tenmile Range along Gore Canyon, several small areas of interlayered felsic gneiss and amphibolite have been recognized. In contrast with the southern Gore Range, only a few small bodies of 1.7-billion-year-old granite occur in the Tenmile and Mosquito Ranges, but several small intrusions of 1.4-billion-year-old granite occur along the Continental Divide near the junction of the ranges.

Perhaps the most important difference between the Gore Range and the ranges to the south is that while the Laramide and post-Laramide igneous rocks that are characteristic of the Colorado Mineral Belt are essentially absent in the Gore Range, they are widespread in both the Tenmile and Mosquito Ranges and in the flanking Paleozoic and Mesozoic sedimentary rocks. These ranges both lie in the Colorado Mineral Belt and bear the scars of a century and a half of mining and prospecting, a fate that the Gore Range largely escaped. Although prospecting and mining are responsible for the network of roads and trails that provide easy access to these mountains, they are also responsible for the patchwork of privately owned patented mining claims, some of whose owners now limit access through their property.

During the Ice Ages, glacial ice draped the ridges and lay deep in the valleys of the Tenmile and northern Mosquito Ranges. Tongues of ice extended down to Breckenridge, and filled the valley of the Blue River all the way to Hoosier Pass; south of the pass, glaciers filled the valley of the Middle Fork of the South Platte all the way to the terminal moraines at Fairplay. Glaciers flowing from an icecap on Fremont Pass completely filled the Tenmile Canyon and deposited terminal moraines that partially encircle the depression that now holds Dillon Reservoir. Another glacier from this ice cap flowed down the East Fork of the Arkansas River to Leadville. Much of the gravel that floors the western part of South Park and the upper Arkansas Valley around Leadville is outwash from these glaciers. South of Weston Pass, the Mosquito Range was essentially ice free.

SAWATCH RANGE

"To the north is a wilderness of peaks, which form the Sawatch range, some capped with igneous rocks, others projecting their ragged, sharp, granitic points or crests high up among the snows, 14,000 feet and upward."

F. V. HAYDEN

7th Annual Report of the U.S. Geological and Geographical Survey of the Territories, 1873

The Sawatch Range extends about eighty-five miles south-southeast from the Eagle River west of Vail to Marshall Pass, just south of Mt. Ouray. The range is flanked on the east by the upper valleys of the Eagle and Arkansas Rivers, and on the west by Taylor Park in the headwaters of the Gunnison River and by lower mountains and ridges in the headwaters of the Roaring Fork that separate it from the Elk Mountains. The Continental Divide follows the crest of the range south of Hagerman Pass, which lies a few miles north of Mt. Massive. The range contains fifteen Fourteeners, more than any other range in Colorado. Although much of it lies in the Colorado Mineral Belt and is laced with old mine roads and prospector's trails, the Sawatch Range also encompasses the Holy Cross, Hunter-Frying Pan, Mount Massive, and Collegiate Peaks Wilderness areas. In the central and southern parts of the range many of the peaks and high ridges tend to be smooth and rounded, so that the alpine scenery is less striking than that of the Gore Range. Notable exceptions include the northern parts of the range around the Mount of the Holy Cross, the Ellingwood Ridge of La Plata Peak, and the area around Ice Mountain and the Three Apostles southwest of Mt. Huron.

The Sawatch Range is carved from a large, elongate upfold or dome (anticline) of basement rocks and the sedimentary strata that overlie them. To picture such a fold, imagine a canoe lying upside down on a beach. The hull of the canoe represents the sedimentary strata in the anticline and the inside of the canoe is filled with the basement rocks that underlie them. The keel of the canoe is the crest of the anticline. Now suppose that you erode the bottom of the canoe, exposing the basement rocks within. The basement rocks would be exposed in an elongate oval area surrounded by an oval belt of the overlying sedimentary rocks. If the canoe is exactly upside down, the sedimentary layers will slope away from the basement rocks on all sides.

This is exactly the pattern we see in the geologic map of the Sawatch Range. The basement rocks (that is, the Precambrian gneisses and granites) crop out in an elongated oval area almost completely surrounded by a belt of Paleozoic sedimentary rocks. The northern end of the basement oval lies just south of the Eagle River between Vail and Eagle; the southern end is largely buried by Tertiary volcanic rocks south of Marshall Pass. The Sawatch anticline began to form about 70 million years ago, in the early stages of the Laramide orogeny. By about 40 million years ago the anticline had been deeply eroded and the cover rocks largely removed, producing the pattern just described. F.V. Hayden (8th Annual Report of the U.S. Geological and Geographical Survey of the Territories, 1874) wrote:

> *"We may safely assert that at some period comparatively modern, 10,000 to 15,000 feet of sedimentary beds extended uninterruptedly from the South Park across the interval now occupied by the Sawatch Range, all of which, but insignificant remnants, have been swept away, while a mass of the granite nucleus of inconceivable dimensions has also been removed.... I find it difficult to estimate the extent of the erosion of this region, and can only speak of it in general terms as almost inconceivable to a finite mind."*

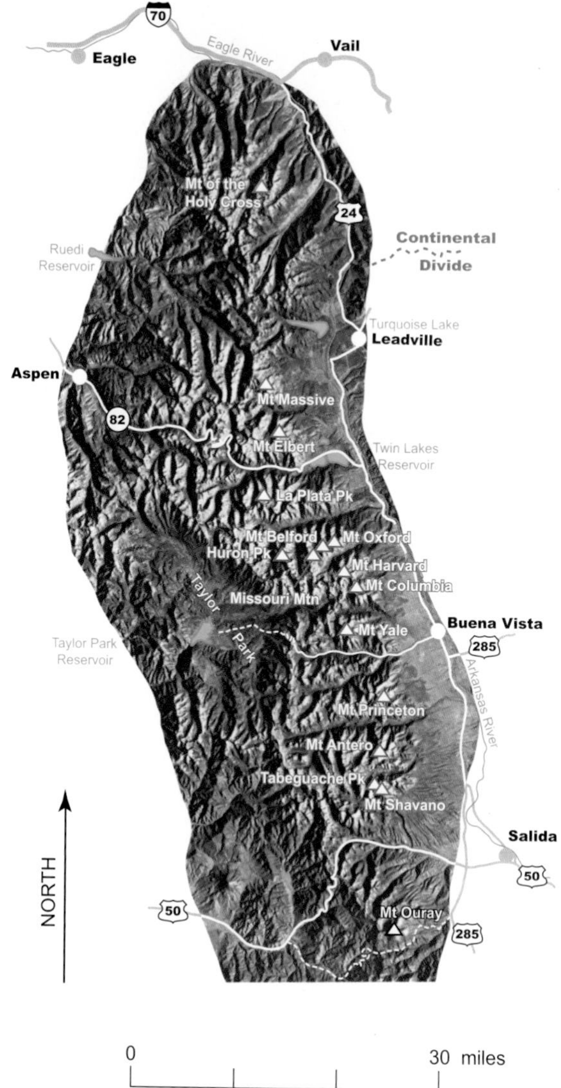

Satellite image of the Sawatch Range showing geographic features.

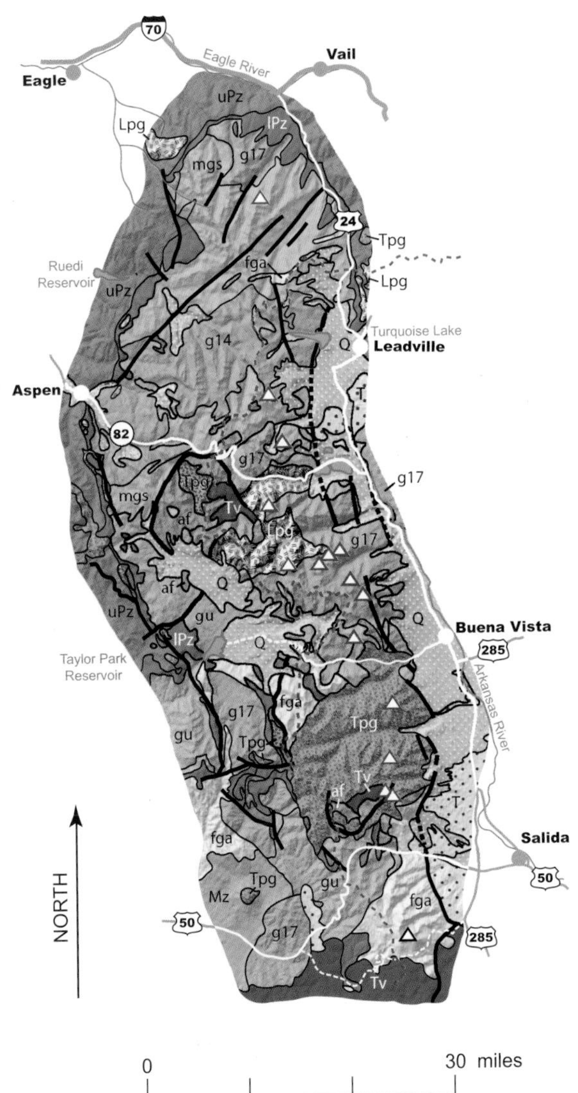

Geologic map of the Sawatch Range.

EXPLANATION

Quaternary deposits
(deposited by streams, glaciers, landslides, or other surficial processes)

Tertiary volcanic rocks

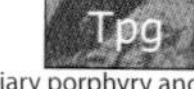

Tertiary porphyry and granite
(intruded after the Laramide orogeny)

Taf

Tertiary ash flows
(deposited in the Grizzly Peak and Mt. Aetna calderas)

Porphyry and granite
(intruded during the Laramide orogeny)

Tertiary sedimentary rocks

Mesozoic sedimentary rocks
(mostly deposited in or near the great Cretaceous seaway)

Upper Paleozoic sedimentary rocks
(mostly deposited during uplift and erosion of the Ancestral Rocky Mountains)

Lower Paleozoic sedimentary rocks
(deposited in shallow seas)

Basement Rocks

Mica gneiss, schist, and migmatite

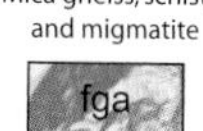

Felsic gneiss and amphibolite

Granite
(age uncertain)

Granite
(intruded about 1.4 billion years ago)

Granite
(intruded about 1.7 billion years ago)

Symbols

Geologic contact

High- angle fault

Thrust fault
(teeth on upper plate)

Explanation for geologic map of the Sawatch Range.

However, there is one complication to this simple picture. About 10 million years ago, the Arkansas Valley segment of the Rio Grande rift began to open and it ultimately split away the southern part of the eastern edge of the eroded anticline. The detached part of its eastern flank now forms the Mosquito Range, and the faults along the western side of the rift now bound the eastern flank of the highest parts of the Sawatch Range, the part that contains all of the Sawatch Fourteeners except Holy Cross.

The Sawatch Range is unique among the Colorado ranges in the abundance and diversity of its granites. Granite of one kind or another comprises at least three quarters of the rock in the core of the range, and includes rocks of at least four different ages. These include widely distributed, irregular bodies of 1.7-billion-year-old granite and a large body of 1.4-billion-year-old granite (both part of the basement), a batholith of granite intruded about 64 million years ago (during the Laramide orogeny), and a batholith intruded about 34 million years ago (after the Laramide orogeny).

In the northern part of the Sawatch Range (north of Colorado Highway 82 between Twin Lakes and Aspen) biotite gneiss, schist, and migmatite are the principal metamorphic rocks in the basement, although layers of amphibolite are also common in some areas. In the vicinity of the Mount of the Holy Cross, the layers in the metamorphic rocks trend roughly north-south or northeast-southwest and are steeply inclined. In this same area there are a number of nearly vertical zones that trend northeast-southwest and in which the rocks have been crushed and recrystallized to a flinty rock called mylonite. These zones formed early in the history of the basement rocks and have subsequently been reactivated several times, most recently during the Laramide orogeny.

The Mount of the Holy Cross. The vertical part of the cross is formed by accumulation of snow in the steep couloir on the northeast face of the mountain. The couloir is formed along a northeast-trending fault in the basement rocks. The horizontal arms of the cross are formed by accumulation of snow on ledges formed along west-sloping joints. The snowy cross commonly disappears in late summer.

RUSS ALLEN PHOTO

The Cross Creek batholith is a large body of streaky 1.7-billion-year-old granite north of the Mount of the Holy Cross and forms Mt. Jackson and Grouse Mountain just south of the Beaver Creek ski area. Many of the runs in the ski area lie on the northeast-sloping beds of lower Paleozoic sedimentary rocks that overlie the granite near the northern end of the Sawatch anticline. Small bodies of similar granite are widespread among the metamorphic rocks in this part of the range.

A large irregular body of 1.4-billion-year-old granite forms a wide northeast-southwest-trending belt across the range from Turquoise Lake near Leadville to the west flank of the range near Aspen. The granite in this body, the St. Kevin batholith, is lighter colored and lacks the conspicuous dark streaks characteristic of the older granite. It makes up much of the northeastern slopes of Mt. Massive,

Mount Princeton and its neighbors are carved in granite of the Mount Princeton batholith and generally have smooth rubble-strewn slopes, except on the walls of glacier-carved canyons, such as that of Chalk Creek. The fault marking the western edge of the Rio Grande rift lies along the foot of the steep mountain slopes.

the Continental Divide around Hagerman Pass, and the spectacular cliffs at Hell Gate along the road west of Hagerman Pass. A narrow irregular belt of biotite gneiss, schist, and migmatite forms the southeast wall of the St. Kevin batholith and forms Mt. Elbert and the northern and southern summit ridges of Mt. Massive.

South of Colorado Highway 82, which runs from Twin Lakes over Independence Pass to Aspen, the geology of the Sawatch Range becomes more complex. The basement rocks in the core of the Sawatch anticline are largely granite, most of which probably belongs to the group of 1.7-billion-year-old granites, but extensive areas in the southwestern parts of the range have not yet been studied in sufficient detail to distinguish the 1.4- from the 1.7-billion-year-old granites. Much of the granite in the central part of the range is rather dark colored and contains large amounts of biotite mica. In many places the biotite is arranged in dark streaks, but in other areas the streaking is lacking. The largest body of this dark granite lies west and northwest of Buena Vista, and from it erosion has carved seven of the Sawatch Fourteeners: La Plata, Oxford, Belford, Missouri, Harvard, Columbia, and Yale. This cluster of peaks, widely known as the Collegiate Range, is the largest constellation of Fourteeners in the Rocky Mountains.

The metamorphic rocks are chiefly felsic gneiss and amphibolite, but a few smaller areas of mica gneiss, schist, and migmatite are scattered throughout the southern part of the range. Around Cottonwood Pass (the pass where the road from Buena Vista to Taylor Park crosses the Continental Divide) the metamorphic rocks include beds of quartzite and conglomerate, rocks that are rare elsewhere in the Colorado Mountains.

Two bodies of much younger granite intrude the basement rocks in the core of the Sawatch anticline. The Twin Lakes batholith, which is located west and southwest of Twin Lakes, consists of light-gray and tan, medium- to coarse-grained granite, locally containing rectangular crystals of gray potassium feldspar several inches long. This granite body was intruded about 65 million years ago, during the early stages of growth of the Sawatch anticline. The deep glaciated canyons of Lake Creek and Clear Creek have been carved in this granite, which seems to have been somewhat less resistant to erosion than the surrounding basement granite in the surrounding high ridges. The projection of the 1.7-billion-year-old granite that forms La Plata Peak is probably part of the roof of the Twin Lakes batholith. Huron Peak lies within the batholith but is partly surrounded by the older granite.

The other young granite body is the Mt. Princeton batholith, which makes up much of the Sawatch Range east of the Continental Divide between the Cottonwood Pass Road and U.S. 50. This batholith is made up chiefly of medium-grained light-gray massive granite, commonly containing scattered larger, pink potassium feldspar crystals. The Chalk Cliffs along Chalk Creek are not chalk at all; they are composed of granite of the Mt. Princeton batholith that has been altered by hot water (like that in the nearby Mt. Princeton Hot Springs) so that the feldspar crystals are transformed into white clay, making the rock so soft that it can be dug with a pocket knife. This soft rock erodes into the awesome spires that decorate the spectacular cliffs. The Mt. Princeton batholith intruded into the surrounding basement rocks 34.3 million years ago, after growth of the Sawatch anticline had largely ceased, but before post-Laramide erosion had destroyed the highlands that the uplift had produced.

Among the high peaks carved from the batholith is (not surprisingly) Mount Princeton, as well as Mount Antero and Mount Shavano. Tabeguache Mountain lies near the southern edge of the batholith with its summit in a narrow wedge of 1.7-billion-year-old granite. The southeastern side of its summit ridge runs in a dike of Mount Princeton granite which contains large, rectangular, white and pink feldspar crystals and large, round grains of gray quartz. Although the summit of Mount Antero lies in granite typical of the Mount Princeton batholith, the southeastern slopes lie in slightly younger and lighter-colored granite. It is this granite that hosts the pegmatite veins and open cavities that contain the crystals of aquamarine and other rare minerals for which the mountain is famous.

The Sawatch Range also displays the scars of two great volcanic depressions known as calderas. Calderas form as the result of the collapse of the roof of a body of molten igneous rock (magma) as it approaches the Earth's surface. As pressure on the magma is suddenly released by the roof collapse, volatile components in the liquid such as water, carbon dioxide, fluorine, and chlorine are suddenly released, causing violent eruptions of huge volumes of molten rock material as volcanic ash. The explosive effect is much like carelessly uncorking a bottle of champagne on top of a Fourteener—a wasteful experiment that you will probably not wish to repeat! These eruptions produce towering eruption clouds that penetrate into the stratosphere. Some of the ash falls back into the depression left by the eruption, but much of it drifts with the wind, sometimes for thousands of miles.

The two Sawatch calderas are the Grizzly Peak caldera west of Twin Lakes and just south of Independence Pass and the Mt. Aetna caldera in the Mt. Princeton batholith just west of Tabeguache Peak. The Grizzly Peak caldera erupted about 34.3 million years ago. The caldera, which is about eighteen miles in diameter, is now filled largely with ash flow tuff, formed by ash that fell back into the depression after the eruption, and with breccia composed of material that avalanched off the caldera walls after the eruption. Most of the fragments in the breccia are angular blocks of granite and gneiss from the surrounding basement rocks and from the Twin Lakes batholith—some of the blocks are tens or hundreds of feet in diameter and the breccia deposits are hundreds of feet thick! The caldera fill is cut by intrusions of light-gray granite with grains of white feldspar and black biotite mica that give it a salt-and-pepper look. This granite probably represents part of the body of molten rock that lay below the caldera prior to the eruption. The volcanic ash that fell outside the caldera has largely been removed by erosion, but one small remnant has been found on the shoulder of Mt. Sopris, thirty miles to the northwest.

The shape and size of the Mt. Aetna caldera are uncertain; only a small down-faulted fragment of its floor is still preserved. It erupted several times about 33.8 million years ago and spread sheets of volcanic ash eastward across the future site of the Rio Grande rift into South Park. The rocks in the preserved fragment of the crater fill include ash flow tuff and breccia like that in the Grizzly Peak caldera, as well as some dark lava and volcanic breccia that were deposited on the land surface before the caldera developed.

As with all of the other great Colorado Ranges, the final shaping of the mountain landscape was the work of Ice Age glaciers. Steve Capps wrote in U.S. Geological Survey Bulletin 386 (1909):

> "...*The ice of the last epoch covered by far the greater parts of these great ranges [the Mosquito and Sawatch]. Here only the narrow crests of the ridges projected above the ice. From this collecting field of snow and ice, which was essentially continuous along the crests of the ranges, the glacial ice moved down the mountains. The ice was deepest and most vigorous in the important mountain valleys, each of which was occupied by a glacier, and ice tongues extended far down the mountain slopes, many of them onto the piedmont plain below. Some of the glaciers consisted of a single lobe, without lateral feeders; others, more favorably situated, were fed by numerous heads, and it was these many-headed glaciers which reached the greatest size and which most profoundly altered the shape of their valleys*..."

In the northern part of the Sawatch Range, north of Tennessee Pass, ice tongues moved down Cross

Creek almost to the Eagle River and down Homestake Creek nearly to Red Cliff. A lobe of the Homestake Glacier at one time blocked the Eagle River, ponding a lake fed by meltwaters from glaciers farther upstream. The bed of this lake forms the flat valley floor at Camp Hale, the training site of the 10th Mountain Division of World War II fame. Farther south, terminal moraines of glaciers that flowed east from the Sawatch Range into the Arkansas Valley form the dams that impound Turquoise Lake, Twin Lakes, and—with a little help from the Bureau of Reclamation–Clear Creek Reservoir. The glaciers from Lake Creek, Clear Creek, and Pine Creek at one time extended completely across the narrowest part of the Arkansas valley, blocking the river and periodically creating ice-dammed lakes. Whenever one of these lakes overtopped the ice dam, the water rapidly cut a channel in the ice, releasing a catastrophic flood. Some of these floods carried boulders as long as sixty-five feet to the outskirts of Buena Vista and as long as thirty feet almost to Salida.

On the west side of the range an ice tongue extended down the Roaring Fork to a terminus several miles north of Aspen. Ice also filled the northern part of Taylor Park, and extended down Texas Creek and Willow Creek to form a lobe that deposited the terminal moraine that encircles Taylor Park Reservoir. All in all, the Ice Age glaciers of the Sawatch Range would have been comparable in size and extent to the modern glaciers of the Mont Blanc massif in the Alps.

THE SANGRE DE CRISTO MOUNTAINS

The Sangre de Cristo Mountains encompass all of the chain of mountains along the eastern flank of San Luis and Rio Grande Valleys from Poncha Pass, south of Salida, to Glorieta Pass, east of Santa Fe, New Mexico, a distance of about 200 miles. Some guidebooks allege that this makes it the longest mountain range in North America, but a glance at the map of Alaska raises considerable doubt. The mountains probably take their name from the color of the upper Paleozoic redbeds that are widespread throughout the entire mountain chain. In Colorado, the Sangre de Cristo Mountains include two distinct ranges: the Sangre de Cristo Range, which includes the mountains between Poncha Pass and La Veta Pass, and the Culebra Range, which extends south from La Veta Pass to the New Mexico state line.

Sangre de Cristo Range

> *"This range rises abruptly from the valley floor to an altitude of 12,000 to 14,000 feet.... Following in its course an almost straight line for forty miles, it presents altogether a very imposing sight. The average width of the Sangre de Christo [sic] Range is not much over ten to twelve miles, which, compared with its length and relative altitude is small, and as the color of the rocks composing it is dark, the range appears to very good advantage.... A naked and sharp appearance is presented by the peaks of this mountain-range. Extending beyond timberline, their highest slopes are composed of loose rocks, usually*

with steep descent into one of the canyons formed at the sides of the highest point."

F. H. ENDLICH

7th Annual report of the U.S. Geological and Geographical Survey of the Territories, 1873

The Sangre de Cristo Range is carved from a block of rocks that was uplifted along normal faults—the Sangre de Cristo fault, which separates it from the San Luis Valley on the west, and the Alvarado fault, which separates it from the Wet Mountain Valley to the east. Uplift of the block between these faults began during initial stages of the opening of the San Luis Valley segment of the Rio Grande rift, approximately 26–27 million years ago, but the main period of rapid uplift occurred about 15 million years ago. Fresh fault scarps along branches of the Sangre de Cristo fault show that uplift along the west side of the range is still continuing. Careful studies of some of the fault scarps indicate that there have been at least two significant earthquakes along these faults in the past 13,000 years. If there is a great earthquake in Colorado's future, the Sangre de Cristo fault is high on the list of candidate sources. The total uplift of the mountain block relative to rocks beneath the floor of the San Luis Valley is estimated to be about 6,500 feet. The two clusters of high peaks in the Sangre de Cristo Range are among the most rugged and spectacular alpine areas in Colorado. The northern cluster includes the Fourteeners Humboldt, Crestone Peak, Crestone Needle, and Kit Carson (as well as Challenger Point, which is included in some lists). The southern cluster

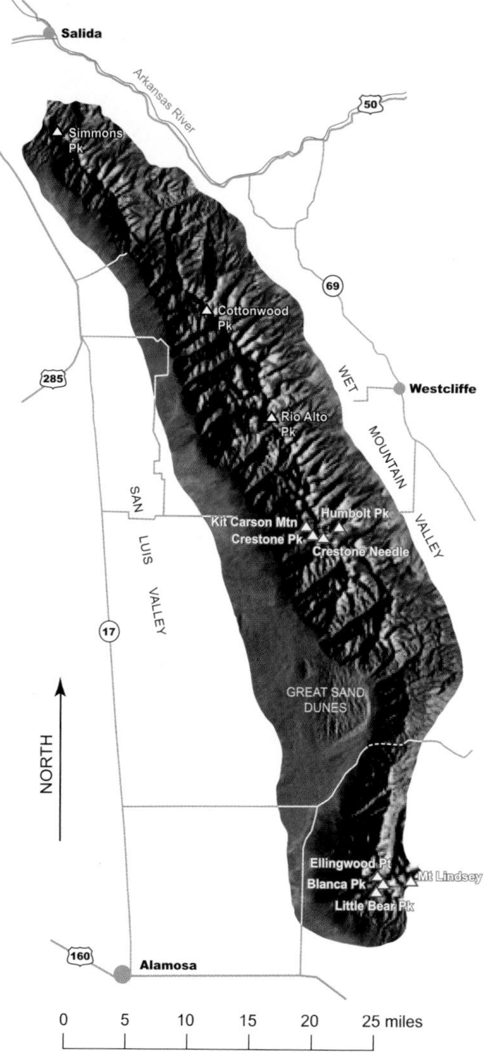

Satellite image of the Sangre de Cristo Range showing geographic features.

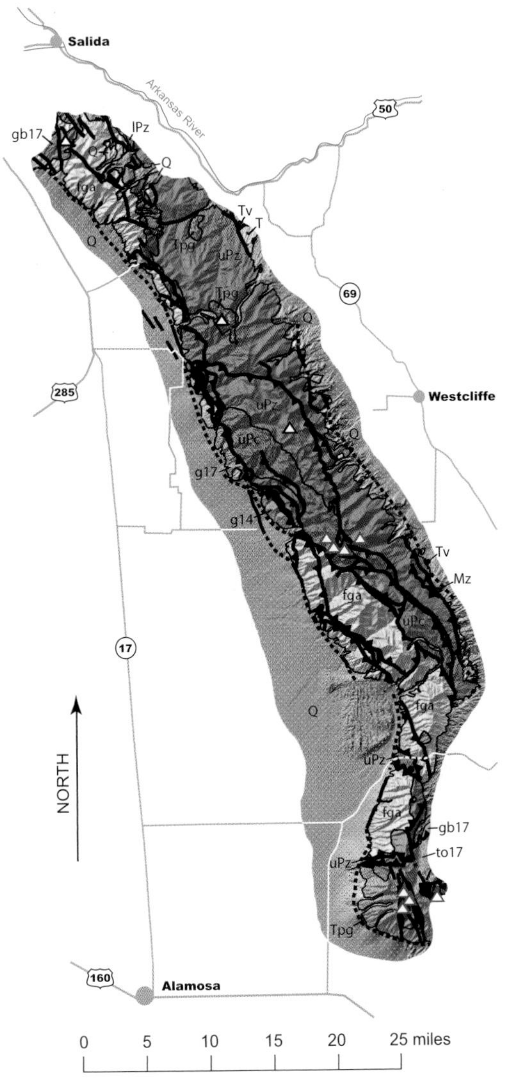

Geologic map of the Sangre de Cristo Range.

EXPLANATION

Quaternary deposits
(deposited by streams, glaciers, landslides,
or other surficial processes)

Tertiary volcanic rocks

Tertiary porphyry and granite
(intruded after the Laramide orogeny)

Tertiary sedimentary rocks

Mesozoic sedimentary rocks
(mostly deposited in or near the great
Cretaceous seaway)

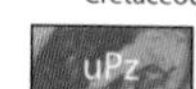

Upper Paleozoic sedimentary rocks
(mostly deposited during uplift and erosion
of the Ancestral Rocky Mountains; uPzc is
Crestone Conglomerate)

Lower Paleozoic sedimentary rocks
(deposited in shallow seas)

Basement Rocks

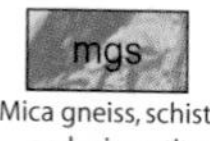

Mica gneiss, schist,
and migmatite

Felsic gneiss and amphibolite

Granite
(intruded about 1.4
billion years ago)

Plutonic rocks intruded about 1.7
billion years ago

Granite

Tonolite

Gabbro

Symbols

Geologic contact

High- angle fault

Thrust fault
(teeth on upper plate)

Explanation for geologic map of the Sangre de Cristo Range.

includes the Fourteeners Blanca, Little Bear, Ellingwood, and Lindsey.

The Sangre de Cristo Range is one of Colorado's most geologically fascinating ranges. The geology of the part of the range that lies north and west of Cottonwood Peak is similar to that of the Mosquito Range. Basement rocks (chiefly felsic gneiss and dark hornblende-rich plutonic igneous rocks) that form the northwestern tip of the range are overlain by east-sloping layers of lower Paleozoic sandstone, limestone and shale, and these sedimentary rocks are in turn overlain by upper Paleozoic gray or red sandstone, shale, and conglomerate on the eastern flank of the range.

Complexly folded and thrust-faulted upper Paleozoic redbeds in the Sangre de Cristo Range. View is south from Venable Peak; peaks on the skyline are Mount Adams (left), Kit Carson Mountain, and unnamed peak 13,546. The strata here lie in a downfold (syncline) in the thrust sheet between the Spread Eagle thrust, which is out of sight behind Mount Adams, and the Sand Creek thrust, which is out of sight behind peak 13,546. The trough of the downfold is visible in unnamed peak 13,153 at the center of the photo. KEN NOLAN PHOTO

Farther south, the main body of the range is made up of upper Paleozoic sedimentary rocks, chiefly red sandstone, conglomerate, and shale, all of which were deposited during the time of the Ancestral Rocky Mountains. Note however, that the geologic map is laced with heavy black lines decorated with small, black saw teeth on one side. The black lines mark the outcrops of thrust faults (moderately

Scrambling on the Crestone Conglomerate. BERNIE HOHMAN PHOTO

to gently inclined faults along which thick sheets of rock above the faults have been carried up and over the rocks below the faults). These thrust faults formed during the Laramide orogeny. The saw teeth on each fault point toward the upper side or "hanging wall" of the fault. Since the trend of the faults on the map is generally about perpendicular to the direction of movement of the rocks in the hanging wall, the saw teeth generally point in the direction opposite to the direction of movement of the hanging wall, except where a thrust fault has itself been folded or faulted by later movements.

These arcane symbols on the geologic map point to an amazing conclusion. During the Laramide orogeny most of the rocks that now make up the Sangre de Cristo Range, including its towering Fourteeners, have been carried northeastward from wherever they originally lay. How far? The width of the thrust sheets shows that some of them have traveled at least five miles, but regional considerations suggest that they may have traveled much farther.

The upper Paleozoic sedimentary rocks that now comprise the main part of the range originally were part of a sequence of layers more than 12,000 feet thick that was deposited in the Central Colorado trough, a lowland that separated the Front Range uplift of the Ancestral Rocky Mountains on the northeast from the Uncompahgre uplift on the southwest. Detailed studies of these rocks show that the streams that carried them from the flanking mountains into the trough flowed generally northeast. The sedimentary rocks in the thrust sheets include a 2,000-foot-thick deposit of very coarse conglomerate that has been mapped for at least twenty-five miles through the heart of the range. The conglomerate (distinguished by a dotted pattern on the geologic map) locally contains cobbles and boulders of various Precambrian basement rocks as much as six feet in diameter. This conglomerate is the rock from which Crestone Peak, Crestone Needle, and Kit Carson are carved. Pebbles, cobbles, and boulders project from the weathered rock faces, forming secure handholds and footholds much appreciated by technical climbers. Clearly such a deposit must have come from the flanks of a major nearby mountain range that lay somewhere to the southwest. The most likely source is the northeastern flank of the late Paleozoic Uncompahgre uplift, which now lies buried beneath the western side of the San Luis Valley. Thus, the thrust sheets that carried the Crestone Conglomerate may have moved twenty-five miles or more northeastward during the Laramide orogeny!

Along the western foot of the range, between Villa Grove and Crestone, thrust faults have carried northeastward slices of Precambrian basement rocks, including felsic gneiss and granite, over upper Paleozoic sedimentary rocks. Small slices of lower Paleozoic rocks have also been carried along some of these faults, notably in the vicinity of Valley View Hot Springs southwest of Cottonwood Peak. South and west of Crestone Peak, a large sheet of Precambrian felsic gneiss and granite has been thrust eastward across the upper Paleozoic sedimentary rocks. Basement rocks in this sheet form the crest of the range east and south of the Great Sand Dunes.

Immediately southeast of the Great Sand Dunes, Mosca Creek has eroded through the sheet of basement rocks to expose the upper Paleozoic sedimentary rocks beneath. This "window" is shown on the geologic map as a small area of sedimentary rocks bounded by thrust faults with saw teeth pointing outward toward the overlying basement rocks.

The cluster of high peaks at the extreme southern end of the range is sometimes referred to as the Sierra Blanca. The rocks there are all igneous, part of the Precambrian basement. Much of this area is occupied by a body of white to very light gray igneous rock called tonalite. The tonalite is composed chiefly of white plagioclase feldspar and quartz, peppered with clots of dark minerals. Quartz and feldspar grains are about the size of BBs; the dark clots are about the size of marbles. The clots were probably originally composed of hornblende and biotite, but these minerals have subsequently been altered to muscovite, chlorite (a green mica-like mineral), and epidote (a pistachio-green mineral). As far as we are aware this is the only body of tonalite that has been found among the Precambrian basement rocks of Colorado. Also in this area are several large bodies of dark hornblende gneiss that were probably formed by metamorphism of plutonic igneous rocks called gabbro or diorite. The summits of Blanca, Little Bear, and Ellingwood are all carved from this type of rock, while the summit of Lindsey is composed of tonalite. The basement rocks in this area are laced with myriad dikes of dark-gray or green Tertiary igneous rocks and cut by numerous faults and fractures. The dikes, faults, and fractures account for the treacherous unstable rocks on the Blanca-Little Bear Ridge and the rock-fall hazards in the couloirs flanking these peaks.

The tonalite and hornblende gneiss of the Sierra Blanca are separated from the basement rocks to the north by thrust faults, but it is not clear whether they themselves are part of a far-traveled thrust sheet. If they are, as seems likely, the source for the unusual tonalite lays hidden deep beneath the young deposits that fill the San Luis Valley.

If you stand atop Little Bear peak and gaze westward across the sere, windswept expanse of the upper San Luis Valley, it is hard to imagine that around half a million years ago this part of the valley was filled with a lake as much as sixty-five miles long and thirty miles wide, and more than one hundred feet deep. Lake Alamosa was formed when lava flows blocked the valley south of Alamosa and persisted for about 3 million years, until it drained catastrophically about 440,000 years ago and cut a channel to join the Rio Grande in northern New Mexico. Its fluctuations record the climate variations during the early part of the Ice Ages. It may well be that winds swept much of the sand that forms the Great Sand Dunes from the dry floor of Lake Alamosa. No doubt the Sangre de Cristo Range supported large glaciers at several times during the existence of Lake Alamosa, but the glaciers, which completed the carving of the modern Sangre de Cristo Range and for which we have direct evidence, developed long after the lake disappeared.

These later Ice Age glaciers carved the U-shaped valleys, polished and striated the rocks on the valley walls and floors, and deposited the moraines that mark the limits of their advances. On the eastern side of the range, ice extended down each of the major valleys. In the lower northern parts of the range, where the valleys drain directly into the Arkansas River, the glaciers were relatively small, and ice did not extend to the mountain front. Farther south, where the peaks are higher and the valleys drain into the Wet Mountain Valley, the glaciers were larger and the ice extended beyond the mountain front and spread out to deposit a coalescing series of terminal moraines along the eastern edge of the range.

Glaciers were much less extensive on the western flank of the Sangre de Cristo Range. Most of the valleys in the northern part of the range were not glaciated. The northernmost significant glacier on the western side extended down Black Canyon, the valley northeast of Cottonwood Peak, nearly to the mountain front. Cotton Creek, about five miles south of Cottonwood Peak, and many of the major valleys to the south, contained glaciers that extended down to the mountain front, where they built conspicuous terminal moraines and spread great fan-shaped deposits of outwash gravel along the eastern side of the San Luis Valley.

The contrast in the extent of the glaciers on the two sides of the range is probably the result of the asymmetry of the range. The drainage divide lies much closer to the steep western slope of the mountains, so that the area above snow line was greater on the eastern side than on the western side. It may also be that, because of its location, the glaciers in the

Sangre de Cristo Range were fed more directly by storms moving up from the Gulf of Mexico rather than by storms coming from the west.

Culebra Range and the Spanish Peaks

Geologically, the Culebra Range is a southern extension of the Sangre de Cristo Range, but down-faulting—along the eastern edge of the Rio Grande rift west of the Culebra Range—took place along a complex series of approximately parallel faults, rather than along a single narrow fault zone like that along the west flank of the Sangre de Cristo Range. Thus, the Culebra Range is flanked on the west by a broad belt of foothills, rather than a precipitous mountain front, like that of its northern neighbor. The Culebra Range contains a dozen or more 13,000-foot peaks, but only one Fourteener, Culebra Peak, which misses by less than nine miles being the highest peak in New Mexico, rather than the forty-first highest in Colorado. Although the range lacks the spectacular alpine scenery of the Sangre de Cristo Range, its more rounded and subdued summits hold many attractions for the mountain hiker. Most of the crest of the range lies on private property, and access is limited and fees are commonly required. However, Trinchera Peak and several of its northern neighbors can be accessed from the east through the San Isabel National Forest.

The eastern flank of the Culebra Range is underlain by complexly folded and thrust-faulted late Paleozoic sedimentary rocks, chiefly gray and red sandstone, shale, and conglomerate. Like the similar rocks along the eastern side of the Sangre de Cristo Range, these sediments are all composed of material eroded from the northeastern flank of the Uncompahgre uplift, one of the major uplifts of the Ancestral Rocky Mountains. The western slopes and foothills are underlain by basement rocks, chiefly 1.7-billion-year-old layered gneiss, schist, hornblende gneiss, and granite, similar to those in the Sangre de Cristo Range. The fault blocks of basement rocks on the east side of the Culebra Range form a series of stair steps that descend westward in the Rio Grande rift. Many of these steps are covered or partly covered by Tertiary sediments and volcanic rocks deposited before or during the early stages of formation of the rift.

The eastern side of the range is separated from the low but rugged hills of Tertiary rocks, which mark the western edge of the High Plains, by a series of narrow north-south-trending valleys occupied by the Cucharas River north of Cucharas Pass and the tributaries of the Purgatoire River south of the pass.

Just as in the Sangre de Cristo Range, the basement rocks in the Culebra Range have been carried eastward across the late Paleozoic sedimentary rocks along thrust faults that formed during the Laramide orogeny. At the same time the sedimentary rocks were pushed eastward and crumpled into folds. North of Francisco Peak, which lies about 4 miles north of Culebra Peak, the crest of the range is entirely in sedimentary rocks. Farther south it is in basement rocks except for a short segment just north of the New Mexico state line, where it is capped by Tertiary volcanic rocks.

Because the Culebra Range is not as high and accumulation areas for ice were smaller, the latest Ice Age glaciers were not as large as those in the Sangre de Cristo Range. Nevertheless, glaciers occupied most of the major valleys in the higher parts of the range. Those on the east side of the range extended down into the foothills to elevations as low as 9,000 feet, and locally coalesced into icefields, the largest of which was as much as a mile wide and seven miles long, extending across the flanks of the higher peaks. Glaciers on the western side were less extensive, and the largest only extended down to elevations of about 9,400 feet. Rock glaciers, which apparently formed after the retreat of the main glacial ice, occupy many of the cirques and some of the flanks of the glacial valleys. Some of the high peaks and ridges that escaped glaciation, and thus have developed a thicker soil blanket, display well-developed stone polygons, which formed by freezing and thawing of the soil during glacial climates.

West Spanish Peak (13,626 feet) and East Spanish Peak (12,683 feet) lie east of the Culebra Range at the western edge of the High Plains. They are not really part of the Sangre de Cristo Mountains, but they are so prominent that they deserve a brief description. They probably represent the roots of volcanoes, but if so, all trace of the volcanic edifice has been removed by erosion, although a small patch of volcanic rocks that may have been derived from the volcanic center has been mapped along the crest of the Culebra Range near La Veta Pass, about twenty miles away. The peaks lie in the northern part of the Raton Basin, the large sediment-filled downwarp that formed along the eastern side of the Culebra Range during the Laramide orogeny. The main mass of the peaks is composed of sandstone, claystone, and shale of Eocene age (between 55 and 35 million years old) that represent the highest layers in the basin fill, but which have largely been removed by erosion, except in the axial part of the northern end of the basin. The summits of the two Spanish Peaks are composed of stocks of gray to brown, granite-like igneous rocks that have baked and hardened the surrounding sediments, making them almost as resistant to erosion as the granitic rocks themselves. Thus, the stocks and their wall rocks stand as prominent peaks, while the surrounding softer sediments have been eroded away. The most distinctive features of the Spanish Peaks are the myriad igneous dikes, some of which radiate from the summit stocks, some of which form an east-northeast-trending swarm, and a few of which have random orientations. The dikes range in thickness from three to as much as one hundred feet, and several are as long as seventeen miles. The largest swarm of radiating dikes is focused on West Spanish Peak and includes more than 500 individual dikes. Because the dikes and their immediate wall rocks are resistant to erosion, they commonly stand as nearly continuous natural walls in the softer sedimentary rocks. The spectacular radiating dike swarms probably developed when the more or less cylindrical bodies of magma in the stocks expanded under high pressure and forced aside the enclosing rocks, thereby forming radiating cracks much like the cracks that form when a pebble hits your windshield. Pictures of the Spanish Peaks and their spectacular dike swarms grace the pages of many a geology textbook.

The stocks and dikes were emplaced in a relatively short interval of time between about 21 and 27 million years ago. This is about the same time as the initiation of rifting along the Rio Grande rift. The erosion that shaped the peaks must have taken place well after 21 million years ago, at the same time as the late uplift and erosion of most of the other Colorado Ranges. Several small cirques on the northern flank of West Spanish Peak were occupied by glaciers, one of which may have extended down to an elevation of 9,000 feet. However, glaciers did not play a major role in sculpting the peaks, probably because they were isolated and had only a very small area above snowline during the Ice Ages. However, the peaks are festooned with a number of small talus slopes and rock glaciers.

THE ELK MOUNTAINS

"The Elk Mountain group is one of the most remarkable ranges in our western Territories, and, so far as my own explorations have extended, is unique in form and structure.

The gorges or cañons cut by Castle and Maroon Creeks are probably without a parallel for ruggedness, depth, and picturesque beauty in any portion of the west. The great variety of colors of the rocks, the remarkable and unique forms of the peaks, and the extreme ruggedness, all combine to impress the beholder with wonder. . . . We see here from 3000 to 5000 feet of stratified rocks lifted up vertically so that the beds are horizontal, or nearly so, presenting to the eye, by the eroded forms, a wilderness of pyramidal cones whose summits rise to a height of 13,000 and 14,000 feet."

F. V. HAYDEN

8th Annual report of the U.S. Geological and Geographical Survey of the Territories, 1876

The Elk Mountains comprise the mountain massif that lies between the Roaring Fork and Crystal Rivers (both tributaries of the Colorado) and extends south and southeast to Taylor Park and the headwaters of the Gunnison River. Geologically, the Elk Mountains lie west of the western flank of the Sawatch Range and southeast of the Grand Hogback (the line of upturned sedimentary strata that separates the Southern Rocky Mountains from the Colorado Plateau). They are putatively the most scenic and almost certainly the most photographed of all the Colorado mountain ranges.

Unlike the Sawatch Range, their neighbor to the east, and the Gore, Mosquito, and Front Ranges, the Elk Mountains are composed largely of sedimentary rocks complexly intruded by large bodies of relatively young igneous rocks. Most of the sedimentary rocks in the range are redbeds—red sandstone, shale, and conglomerate—that resemble those in the Sangre de Cristo Mountains. They rest on older Paleozoic sedimentary strata, chiefly sandstone, shale, and limestone deposited in the shallow, early Paleozoic seas that once covered most of Colorado. These older strata are exposed in a narrow belt along the southeastern flank of the range, where they host the silver, lead, and zinc deposits that led to the founding of Aspen, around the southern end of the

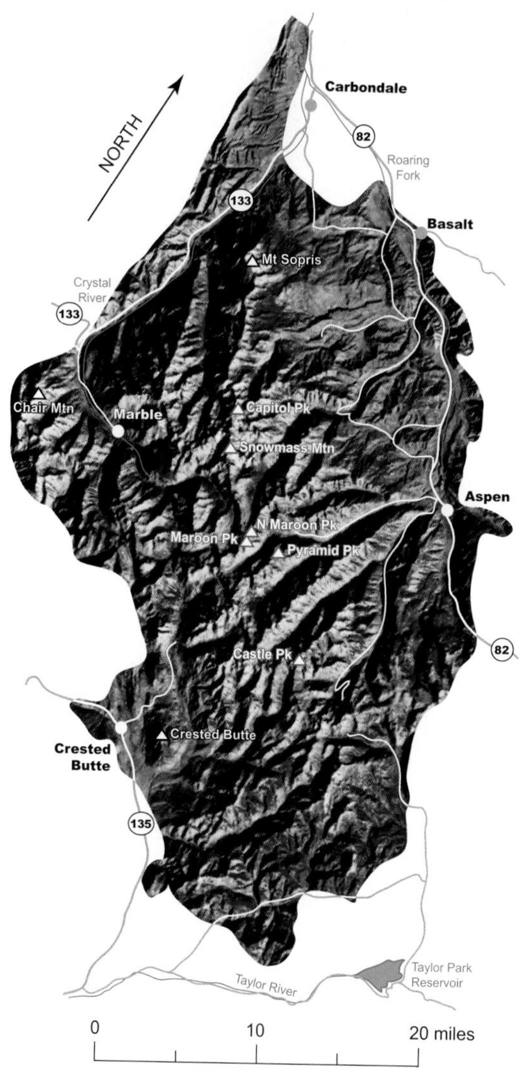

Satellite image of the Elk Mountains showing geographic features.

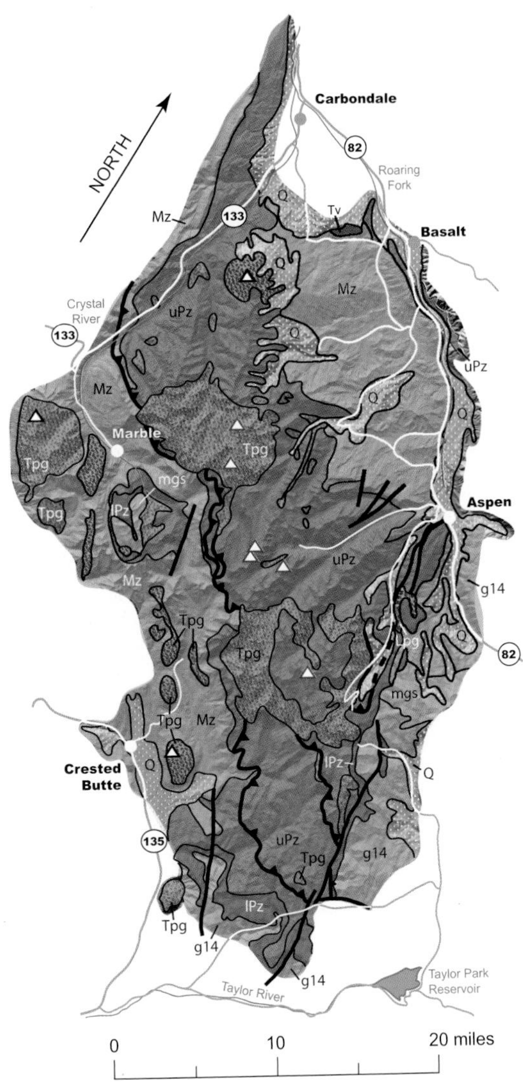

Geologic map of the Elk Mountains.

EXPLANATION

Quaternary deposits
(deposited by streams, glaciers, landslides, or other surficial processes)

Tertiary volcanic rocks

Tertiary porphyry and granite (intruded after the Laramide orogeny)

Porphyry and granite (intruded during the Laramide orogeny)

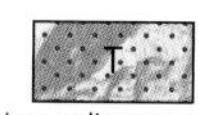

Tertiary sedimentary rocks

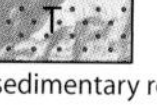

Mesozoic sedimentary rocks (mostly deposited in or near the great Cretaceous seaway)

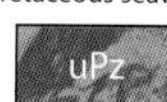

Upper Paleozoic sedimentary rocks (mostly deposited during uplift and erosion of the Ancestral Rocky Mountains)

Lower Paleozoic sedimentary rocks (deposited in shallow seas)

Basement Rocks

Mica gneiss, schist, and migmatite

Granite (intruded about 1.4 billion years ago)

Symbols

Geologic contact

High-angle fault

Thrust fault (teeth on upper plate)

Explanation for geologic map of the Elk Mountains.

range. They are also apparent in a small dome-shaped uplift in the headwaters of the Crystal River, where limestone in the upper part of the sequence has been metamorphosed by an igneous intrusion into the world famous Yule Marble.

During the rise of the Ancestral Rocky Mountains, 300 to 250 million years ago, the future site of the Elk Mountains lay in the Central Colorado trough, a narrow lowland flanked by the Ancestral Front Range highlands to the northeast and the Ancestral Uncompahgre highland to the southwest. At times parts of this trough were occupied by shallow seaways, but as the adjacent highlands grew, more than two miles of sand, clay, silt, and gravel accumulated in the intervening trough within broad floodplains and alluvial fans. Trunks of tree ferns are found in these deposits near Minturn, and recently, slabs of rock containing tracks of amphibians or reptiles that wandered these hot, tropical mudflats have been discovered near Pyramid Peak. The red color of these rocks is due to oxidation of iron minerals exposed to air and groundwater under desert or near-desert conditions, probably much like the conditions that now prevail around the head of the Gulf of California. Conglomerate composed of pebbles washed in from the Uncompahgre Highland are common, but there are no large bodies of very coarse boulder conglomerate like those in the northern Sangre de Cristo Range. The contrast between the solid conglomerate faces studded with comfortable holds on Crestone Needle and Crestone Peak and the treacherous loose and rotten rock on the Maroon Bells is obvious to any climber, although the rocks are the same age and were deposited under similar conditions.

Interlayered red sandstone and shale of the upper Paleozoic Maroon Formation exposed on the east face of the Maroon Bells. The beds slope ten to fifteen degrees to the north. The lowermost beds in the photo are bleached to white in the contact zone around a body of granite that lies buried in the valley of Maroon Creek, between the Maroon Bells and Pyramid Peak.

By about 200 million years ago (early in the Mesozoic era), the Ancestral Rocky Mountain uplifts had been entirely destroyed by erosion and thin layers of siltstone; limestone deposited in shallow lakes and sluggish streams covered the site of the Central Colorado trough. Between about 110 and 75 million

Negotiating (rather inelegantly) the famous Knife Edge on Capitol Peak. The rock is complexly jointed granite of the 34-million-year-old Snowmass stock. KARL KELLOGG PHOTO

years ago, much of Colorado was submerged beneath the waters of a great Cretaceous seaway. More than a mile of mud, sand, and lime-rich sediment (later consolidated to form shale, sandstone, and limestone) were deposited on the older sedimentary rocks in the area that was to become the Elk Mountains.

The seaway began to retreat eastward about 70 million years ago, during the early stages of the Laramide orogeny. In fact, the withdrawal of the seaway was probably due to the first stirrings of Laramide uplift. The area of the Elk Mountains rose initially as part of the Sawatch anticline. The thick prism of Late Paleozoic sediments filling the Central Colorado trough was uplifted and folded into a series of anticlines and synclines. During the later stages of the orogeny a thick sheet of late Paleozoic redbeds, including almost all of the sedimentary rocks now exposed between Aspen and the crest of the range was shoved ten miles or more westward and southwestward along a series of gently eastward-inclined thrust faults, the westernmost of which is known as the Elk Range thrust. At the leading edge of the thrust, northeast and east of Marble, the late Paleozoic redbeds overrode the sedimentary strata deposited in the Cretaceous seaway. All the rock layers below the leading edge of the southwest-moving thrust were folded back on themselves and overturned toward the southwest. Layers of rock above the thrust, chiefly redbeds from the Ancestral Rockies, were bent downward near the thrust and also overturned toward the southwest. In his report cited above, Hayden (1876) wrote:

> *"On the west side of the Elk Mountains the confusion is still greater, producing not only the most remarkable faults of all the western country, but literally overturning thousands of feet of strata."*

It has been suggested that the Elk Range thrust is the result of gravity sliding a thick package of rocks off the west side of the rising Sawatch anticline. However, the thrust dies out to the northwest and passes into the sharp fold of the Grand Hogback, indicating that it is probably a deep-seated structure more like the thrust fault along the west side of the Laramide Front Range uplift that carries basement rocks westward across Cretaceous and younger strata. Shortly after the Elk Range thrust sheet was emplaced, its trailing edge was broken by the Castle Creek fault, a steeply easterly inclined fault that extends north down the valley of Castle Creek to Aspen and then northeast down the Roaring Fork to near Basalt. The Castle Creek fault marks the boundary between the Sawatch Range and the Elk Mountains. Along it the basement rocks and overlying early Paleozoic rocks of the Sawatch anticline were carried up and westward relative to the rocks of the Elk Mountains. Both the Elk Range and Castle Creek faults must have formed before 67 million years ago, because that is the age of small bodies of igneous rock that were intruded into the Castle Creek fault after it had ceased moving.

By the end of the Laramide uplift in this region, about 65 million years ago, a highland extended all the way from Aspen to Fairplay (the Rio Grande rift, which forms the Arkansas valley, had not yet developed). However, by the middle of the Eocene, about

45 million years ago, the upland had been reduced by erosion to a landscape of low hills and broad valleys, and probably stood at a much lower elevation.

At the beginning of the Oligocene, about 34 million years ago, a major episode of igneous activity flared up, affecting much of central and southwestern Colorado. In many areas molten rock material reached the surface and erupted in volcanoes. Except for one small area on Mt. Sopris, there is no evidence that any volcanic rocks were erupted in the Elk Mountains, but large volumes of granite magma were injected into the already deformed sedimentary rocks throughout much of the range. The granite is a white to light-gray rock made up largely of grains of quartz, feldspar, biotite and/or hornblende that range in size from that of a grain of sugar to that of a small grain of rice. The granite is somewhat finer grained than most of the Precambrian basement granites and lacks the streaky appearance that many of them display. It forms several large, irregular bodies, one around Mt. Sopris, one around Snowmass Mountain and Capitol Peak, and a large, irregular sheet-like body that crops out in an asymmetric ring centered near Castle Peak. These bodies cut through the Elk Range thrust and the other thrust faults, showing that the faults formed before the granite was intruded. Because the magma was intruded at searing temperatures (more than 1100°F), it metamorphosed many of the enclosing rocks, changing the sandstone to quartzite and the shale to a tough, hard, light-greenish-gray rock called hornfels. The high temperatures and hot solutions associated with the intrusions also bleached many of the adjacent maroon rocks, altering them to white or shades of gray. The great volume of granite injected into the sedimentary rocks may have raised the Eocene land surface by as much as 3,000 or 4,000 feet. Both the granitic bodies and the quartzite and hornfels are very resistant to erosion and tend to form high peaks. Snowmass Mountain, Capitol Peak, and Mt. Sopris are made up largely of granite; Castle and Cathedral Peaks are chiefly hornfels. The beds of shale and sandstone on the lower slopes of the Maroon Bells and Pyramid Peak have been altered by the granite intrusions, but those in the higher parts of these peaks are not appreciably affected—perhaps this contributes to the notoriously unstable and treacherous nature of the rocks on the upper slopes of these peaks.

A second episode of granite injection took place about 30 million years ago, close on the heels of the initial one. The younger granite characteristically contains rectangular crystals of pink potassium feldspar, some as long as two inches, in a finer grained matrix that resembles the old granite. The younger granite forms dikes that crosscut the older rocks as well as sheet-like bodies a few feet to thousands of feet thick parallel or almost parallel to beds in the sedimentary rocks or to faults such as the Elk Range thrust. It also forms flat-bottomed pillow-like bodies called laccoliths—these are common in the Mesozoic rocks southwest of the Elk Range thrust fault. Mountains such as Chair Mountain and Crested Butte are carved from laccoliths of the younger granite that have been stripped of their cover of soft, less resistant sedimentary rocks.

Since the intrusion of the main bodies of granite and the uplift associated with them, the area of the Elk Range has been affected by the same rapid uplift as the other Colorado ranges. During the last 5 million years or so the entire region has been uplifted, perhaps by thousands of feet. In the valley of the Roaring Fork near Woody Creek, a basalt flow dated at about 1.4 million years rests on a deposit of gravel that must have been deposited by the Roaring Fork. The gravel now stands about 1,200 feet above the river, indicating that the river has cut down at least that much since the basalt was erupted. The average rate of down-cutting (and presumably the rate of regional uplift) thus would have been about one inch per century.

As in most other parts of the Colorado mountains, glaciers played a major role in shaping the present landscape. During the latter parts of the Ice Ages, glaciers occupied all of the major mountain valleys. Glaciers in the valleys of Maroon Creek, Conundrum Creek, Castle Creek, and Hunter Creek merged with the glaciers flowing down the Roaring Fork valley from the Sawatch Range to form an ice tongue that extended down-valley to a terminus about three miles north of Aspen. Ice also filled the valleys of Snowmass Creek and Capitol Creek, but did not extend all the way to the Roaring Fork.

The last major glaciers disappeared about 12,000 years ago, but since then the landscape has been shaped by avalanches, rock falls, and debris flows as well as by stream erosion. Although they are common in most Colorado ranges, rock glaciers are particularly abundant in the Elk Range. These lobate tongues of talus and scree have the shape and appearance of small glaciers, but no ice is visible at their surfaces, although they probably have cores of ice. Most of them have clearly formed since the retreat of the last Ice Age glaciers, for they lie in cirques or on valley walls that were shaped by the glaciers. Many rock glaciers are no longer active, as is shown by the growth of lichens and plants on them. However, some are still moving—measurements in the 1960s show that rock glaciers on North Maroon and Pyramid Peaks are still moving at rates of as much as two feet per year. Detailed studies of the abundant rock glaciers on Mt. Sopris suggest that they all formed within about the last 5,000 years, after an interval of warm climate that followed the disappearance of the Ice Age glaciers. Some may have formed during the Little Ice Age, an interval of unstable climate with many cold periods between about 1300 and 1850 AD. The ice in the rock glaciers is probably not fossil ice from the main Ice Age glaciers, but ice formed from surface water that trickles into the talus and freezes where it is protected by the blanket of rubble.

THE SAN JUAN MOUNTAINS

"The great and essential differences in topography resulting from the change of geological formation is here so very marked and is so very interesting that I cannot pass it by without comment."

FRANK RODA
Hayden Survey, 1874.

The San Juans are the largest, most varied, and among the most scenic mountain groups in Colorado. They are not a single mountain range, but a collection of named and unnamed ranges and sub-ranges, each with its own character and distinctive geologic story. By far the largest part of this great mountain edifice is carved from volcanic rocks, remnants of a vast volcanic field that blanketed much of the area of the southern Rocky Mountains between about 37 and 23 million years ago, well after the close of the Laramide orogeny. In the San Juan volcanic field alone, almost 10,000 cubic miles of volcanic rocks are preserved, and small remnants of the volcanic blanket are found in the northern Front Range, in the Sawatch Range, and in the West Elk Mountains.

Along the western edge of the San Juans, the mountains carved in volcanic rocks are flanked by ranges of entirely different character formed by totally different rocks. These include the Needle Mountains, which are composed entirely of basement rocks, and the San Miguel Mountains, which are composed mostly of young, dark- to medium-gray igneous rocks that intruded and baked Mesozoic and younger sedimentary rocks beneath the volcanic pile.

Northwestern Volcanic San Juan Mountains

The volcanic rocks of the San Juan Mountains rest on and partly conceal two basement cored uplifts that were formed during the Laramide orogeny: the San Luis uplift on the northeast and the San Juan dome, a more or less circular uplift centered in the Needle

Mountains on the southwest. In this discussion we focus only on the northwestern part of the volcanic field, essentially the part north and west of Creede, because this part contains all of the highest peaks.

Along the western and northwestern margins of the volcanic field the volcanic rocks overlie Mesozoic rocks, chiefly black shale and red and white sandstone (*Mz* on the geologic map) which have been intruded by stocks and laccoliths of porphyry and granite (*Lpg* on the geologic map) during the Laramide orogeny. The Mesozoic sedimentary rocks and the Laramide intrusions are separated from the volcanic rocks by the Telluride Conglomerate, locally as much as 1,000 feet thick, which formed from gravel that accumulated in stream valleys cut into the soft Mesozoic rocks during post-Laramide erosion of the flanking uplifts. This conglomerate layer (*Ts* on the geologic map) forms the cliff down which Bridal Vail Creek plunges to form the famous falls east of Telluride.

Volcanism began about 35 million years ago with the eruption of dark- to medium-gray lava with relatively low silica, or quartz, content from several dozen volcanoes scattered throughout the region. These volcanoes may have resembled the active volcanoes of the present Cascade Range in Washington and Oregon. The volcanic cones were built of lava flows and explosively ejected volcanic debris in fragments ranging in size from boulders tens of feet in diameter to dust-sized shards of volcanic glass ejected as volcanic ash. As the cones were being built, they were being rapidly eroded by streams and mudflows, which carried volcanic debris downslope to

Satellite image of the northwestern San Juan Mountains showing geographic features.

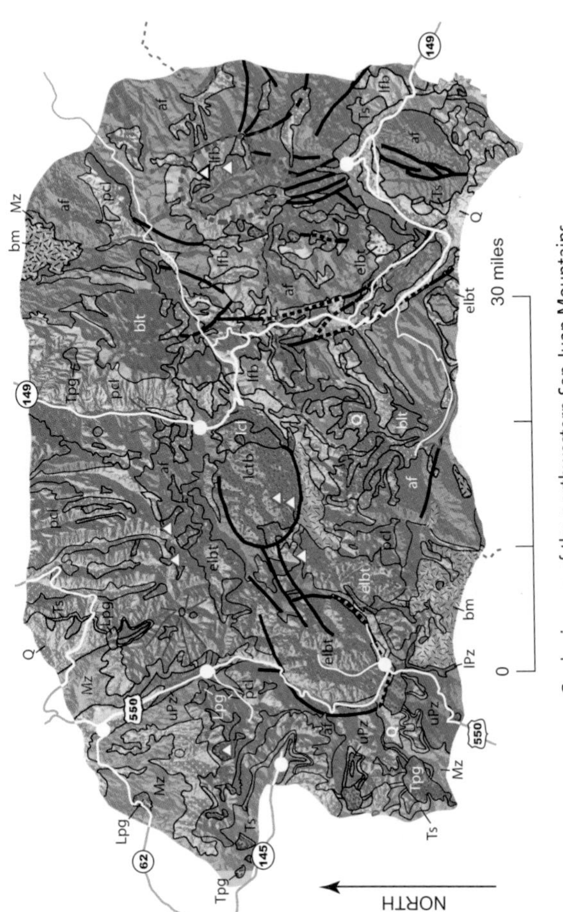

Geologic map of the northwestern San Juan Mountains.

EXPLANATION

Ts

Tertiary sedimentary rocks (Telluride Conglomerate in western part of map; Creede Formation around Creede caldera)

Pre-volcanic rocks

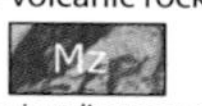

Mesozoic sedimentary rocks (mostly deposited in or near the great Cretaceous seaway)

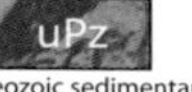

Upper Paleozoic sedimentary rocks (mostly deposited during uplift and erosion of the Ancestral Rocky Mountains)

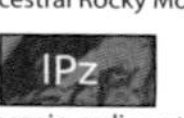

Lower Paleozoic sedimentary rocks (mostly deposited in shallow seas)

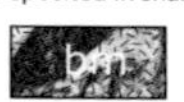

Basement rocks (granite and metamorphic rocks)

Rocks of the San Juan volcanic field

Lava flows and breccia interlayered with ash flow tuff

af

Ash flow tuffs erupted from various calderas between 29 and 23 million years ago

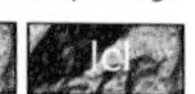

Rocks formed during collapse of Lake City caldera about 23 million years ago. lctb, tuff and breccia; lcl, light colored lava along caldera rim

Dark lava, breccia, and tuff deposited during collapse of early calderas about 28.2 million years ago

Pre-caldera lava, conglomerate and breccia deposited between 33 and and 30 million years ago

Other rocks and surficial deposits

Q

Quaternary deposits (Young materials deposited by streams, landslides, and glaciers)

blt

Basalt erupted between 26 and 14 million year ago

Tpg

Tertiary porphyry, granite, and other rocks (intruded after the Laramide orogeny)

Lpg

Porphyry and granite intruded during the Laramide orogeny

Symbols

Geologic contact

Fault

Dikes

Outline of Nelson Mountain caldera

Explanation for geologic map of the northwestern San Juan Mountains.

build large fan-shaped aprons around and between the individual volcanoes. Where the fragments in these deposits are angular, the material is called volcanic breccia; where the fragments are rounded it is described as volcanic conglomerate. It has been estimated that these early volcanic rocks (*pcl* on the geologic map) covered an area of about 10,000 square miles and comprise about two thirds of the total volume of the entire San Juan volcanic field.

About 29 million years ago a different type of volcanism began in the San Juans. This new activity involved the formation of at least a dozen large calderas, similar to but slightly younger than those in the Sawatch Range. Three of these—the 27.6-million-year-old Silverton caldera north of Silverton, the 26.7-million-year-old Creede caldera south of Creede, and the 23-million-year-old Lake City caldera southwest of Lake City—are clearly visible as circular patterns both on the satellite image and on the geologic map. Older calderas are harder to see; many of them have been partly obliterated by the collapse of younger calderas or have been largely concealed by ejecta from younger eruptions. For example, the Silverton and Lake City calderas are both nested within the older Uncompahgre and San Juan calderas, neither of which is shown on the map. The Creede caldera, the 27-million-year-old Nelson Mountain caldera, and several others are nested within the older La Garita caldera (not distinguished on the map), which is by far the largest caldera recognized—more than forty miles long and twenty-five miles across! This single eruption produced almost

2,000 cubic miles of volcanic ash, and was among the largest volcanic eruptions known on Earth.

Most of the material ejected by a caldera eruption is volcanic ash—broken shards of volcanic glass formed by solidification of frothy lava produced by explosive pressure release during the eruption. Much of the ash in the eruption cloud falls back into the caldera, partly or completely filling it. Both the Creede and Lake City calderas are filled with ash generated during the eruptions that formed them.

However, much of the ash in the eruption cloud is spread across the surrounding landscape as huge moving sheets of hot volcanic ash called ash flows. An ash flow can travel at speeds of eighty to one-hundred miles per hour, engulfing everything before it, filling valleys and even flowing across ridges and other topographic obstructions. When an ash flow comes to rest it forms a sheet of tuff (consolidated volcanic ash) that may be as much as several hundred feet thick near its source but which gradually thins out away from the source. Some ash flows in the San Juans have traveled as much as sixty miles from their source calderas. Some were so hot that when they came to rest the glass shards welded together forming a hard glassy rock called welded tuff. On the geologic map, ash flow tuffs from all the calderas are grouped together as a single map unit (*af* on the map). The area covered by ash flow tuffs in the San Juans is comparable to that covered by the earlier volcanic rocks, but the total volume of the ash flows is only about half that of the deposits from the central volcanoes.

Between about 26 and 25 million years ago, shortly after the collapse of the Silverton and Creede calderas, the volcanic rocks were invaded by stocks and irregular bodies of intrusive igneous rocks composed of porphyry, dark gray granite, and gabbro in various proportions (*Tpg* on the map). Because these rocks tend to be relatively resistant to erosion, many of these bodies stand out as prominent ridges or spires. Mt. Sneffels and Matterhorn Peak are both carved from small stocks of these intrusive rocks that were intruded into the pre-caldera lavas. Some or all of these bodies may have fed large volcanoes that have long since been eroded away. The dark-gray and brown lava flows and associated volcanic conglomerate and breccia that make up Uncompahgre Peak may have been erupted from one of these

The jagged eastern summit ridge of Mount Sneffels is carved in intrusive rocks of the Sneffels stock. Mountains beyond the ridge are composed of horizontally layered volcanic rocks, chiefly pre-caldera lava, breccia, and conglomerate, but the upper few hundred feet of the highest ridges are capped by ash flow tuffs erupted from some of the early calderas.

volcanoes. Recent studies indicate that many of the mineral veins in the rich gold-silver deposits of the San Juan mining districts were formed by the action of hot solutions associated with these 26-to-25-million-year-old intrusions, but some are also related to later intrusions. In the mineralized areas the hot ore-bearing solutions have oxidized iron-rich minerals in the rocks to produce the spectacular red, orange, and yellow colors for which the San Juan Mountains are famous.

The eruption of the Lake City caldera about 23 million years ago marked the end of the explosive caldera-forming volcanic activity in the San Juan volcanic field. The Lake City caldera is almost completely filled with tuff and interleaved breccia formed from collapse of the caldera walls as it subsided (*lctb* on the map). Redcloud and Sunshine Peaks are both carved in this tuff. Nearby Handies Peak is carved in breccia, dark lava, and tuff that filled the older San Juan and Uncompahgre calderas,

Red Mountain No. 3 and its neighbors northwest of Silverton. The brilliant colors tell of the rich mineral deposits on their slopes.

GEORGE MOORE PHOTO

but which probably was uplifted during formation of the Lake City caldera.

By the end of the explosive volcanic activity the landscape in the main part of the San Juans was a slightly eroded plateau formed largely of ash flow tuffs above which stood some of the older eroded volcanic cones and hills cored by resistant intrusive igneous rocks. Parts of the Precambrian basement rocks (*bm* on the map) that formed the core of the old San Juan dome were never buried by volcanic rocks and stood as mountains above the plateau surface. At that time, the Continental Divide probably lay just west of the Creede caldera. In the center of the Creede caldera, a circular dome had been pushed up by rising magma shortly after the caldera formed, producing a horseshoe-shaped depression between the rising dome and the western, northern, and eastern parts of the caldera rim. This depression was occupied by Lake Creede, a deep saline lake, which had no outlet during much of its existence, but which occasionally rose high enough to spill eastward into the ancestral Rio Grande.

As streams cut down into the volcanic plateau, they carved valleys a few hundred feet deep, some of which flowed north and northwest into the Gunnison River and some east or southeast into the Rio Grande. As these valleys were being excavated, flows of basalt (unit *blt* on the map) unrelated to the previous volcanism were erupted, veneering parts of the plateau surface and filling some of the valleys to depths of several hundred feet. The eruption of most of these lava flows took place over an interval of about 10 million years, beginning at about 24 million years ago.

Thus they provide a rough marker from which to measure the subsequent deformation of the old plateau surface.

Erosion of the plateau continued during eruption of the lava flows and continued at a relatively slow rate for the next 7 or 8 million years, gradually increasing the depths of the valleys and reducing the uplands that stood above the plateau surface. However, about 5 million years ago the San Juan region was rapidly uplifted during the same regional uplift that affected most of the other ranges in the Colorado Rockies. At the same time, the plateau surface was tilted gently eastward, toward the newly forming Rio Grande rift. Today the plateau surface is at an altitude of about 7,800 feet along the Rio Grande rift at the eastern edge of the mountains. In the western San Juans, near Silverton and Ouray, its altitude is about 13,800 feet, as projected from preserved remnants of the basalt veneer on the plateau surface. Thus the old surface has been tilted so that it is more than a mile lower on the east than on the west. This probably accounts for the fact that all but one of the 14,000-foot peaks in the San Juans lie in the western part of the massif—the single exception is San Luis Peak.

The regional uplift caused all of the major streams to deepen their valleys, forming deep, alpine canyons. The eastward tilt caused the eastward flowing streams to cut more rapidly and to extend headward into the plateau. Coincidentally, about 5 million years ago, movement along the northeast-trending faults west of the Creede caldera cut through the Continental Divide and allowed the headwaters of rejuvenated Rio Grande to cut rapidly westward to intercept some of the streams that originally flowed into the Gunnison and divert them east into the Rio Grande. This stream capture took place sometime after 5 million years ago. It shifted about 600 square miles from Pacific drainage into Atlantic drainage and caused the large embayment in the Continental Divide west of Creede. The Colorado Trail follows the newly established Continental Divide for many miles west and north of Creede.

At the same time, the increased flow in the Rio Grande caused the river to cut down the outlet of Lake Creede, draining the lake and exposing the sediments deposited in it. These sediments, which form the Creede Formation, are shown as *Ts* on the geologic map, even though they are much younger than the Telluride Conglomerate.

During the Pleistocene, glaciers and icefields in the San Juans covered an area of more than 5,000 square miles. The largest icefields and glaciers were developed in the western part of the range, because of the eastward tilting of the plateau surface. An icefield centered southeast of Silverton covered all but the highest peaks of the Needle Mountains and fed large valley glaciers that extended many miles down all the major valleys. The glacier in the valley of the Uncompahgre River extended beyond Ridgway, the one down the Animas nearly to Durango, and the one down the Rio Grande almost to Creede. Other smaller icefields fed extensive valley glaciers in the central and southeastern parts of the range.

During the glacial advances, treeline lay 2,000 feet or more below its present altitude (11,000 to 11,500 feet). Studies of tree rings, dating of wood fragments, and studies of pollen in cores taken from lakes and bogs indicate that the elevation of timberline continued to fluctuate after the retreat of the glaciers. Between 9,600 and 5,400 years ago treeline was at least 250 feet higher than it is today; between 5,400 and 3,500 years ago it was near its present altitude; and after 3,500 years ago it was generally lower than its present altitude.

The San Juans are festooned with one of the largest arrays of rock glaciers in the conterminous U.S—more than 650 have been mapped. They form in high-altitude talus accumulations in which water trickles down and freezes between the talus blocks.

Mount Sneffels and its neighbors stand at the eroded northwestern edge of the San Juan volcanic plateau. Sneffels and the unnamed peak 12,910 in the right foreground are carved in intrusive rocks of the Sneffels stock. Cirque Mountain on the left skyline is carved in horizontally layered volcanic rocks. Notice the enormous rock glaciers that extend down the valleys from Cirque Mountain.

DOUG RICHARDS PHOTO

Some have ice cores, probably formed from snow accumulations that have been buried in talus. Some of them are more than a mile long. They move downslope at rates of a few inches a year, due to flowage of the interstitial ice, which flows much like the ice in a true glacier.

Needle Mountains

The Needle Mountains, which form the southwestern part of the San Juan mountain complex, are among the most rugged ranges in Colorado. They include many sharp peaks over 13,000 feet, and four 14,000-foot peaks and precipitous south-draining canyons, including the canyons of the Los Pinos River, Vallecito Creek, and the Animas River. Unlike other parts of the San Juans, the Needle Mountains are comprised almost entirely of Precambrian basement rocks in the core of a dome-shaped uplift that formed during the Laramide orogeny and that was never covered by the thick blanket of young volcanic rocks of the San Juan volcanic field. Although they are geographically part of the San Juans, this difference in geology results in a different feel to the mountain landscape. The basement rocks are overlain by ash-flow tuff and volcanic breccia along the northeastern flank of the range and by outward-tilted Paleozoic sedimentary rocks along the western, southwestern, and southern flanks. The lower part of the Paleozoic sequence consists of a hundred feet of gray limestone, shale, and sandstone. The upper Paleozoic rocks are chiefly red or gray sandstone, shale, and siltstone composed at least in part of materials eroded from the Uncompahgre uplift of the Ancestral Rocky mountains.

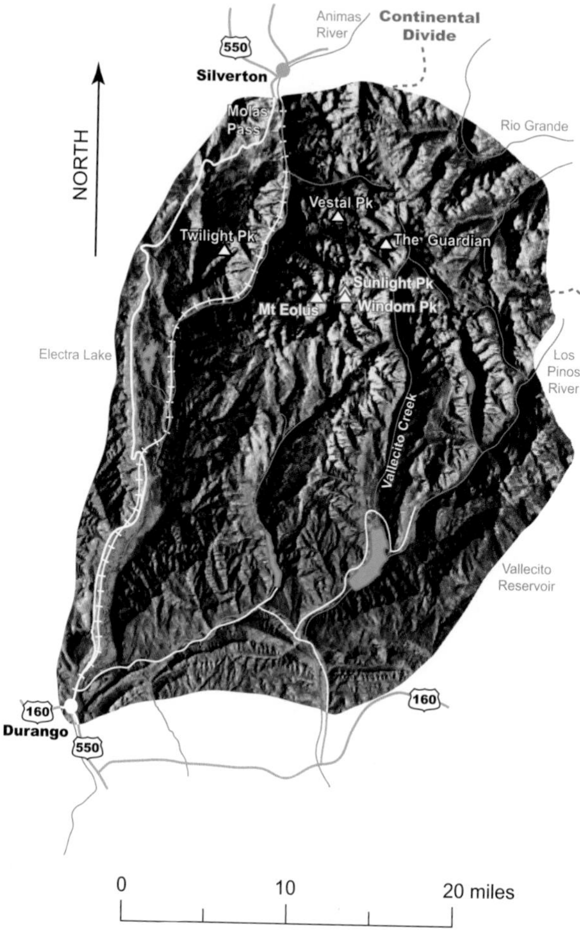

Satellite image of the Needle Mountains showing geographic features.

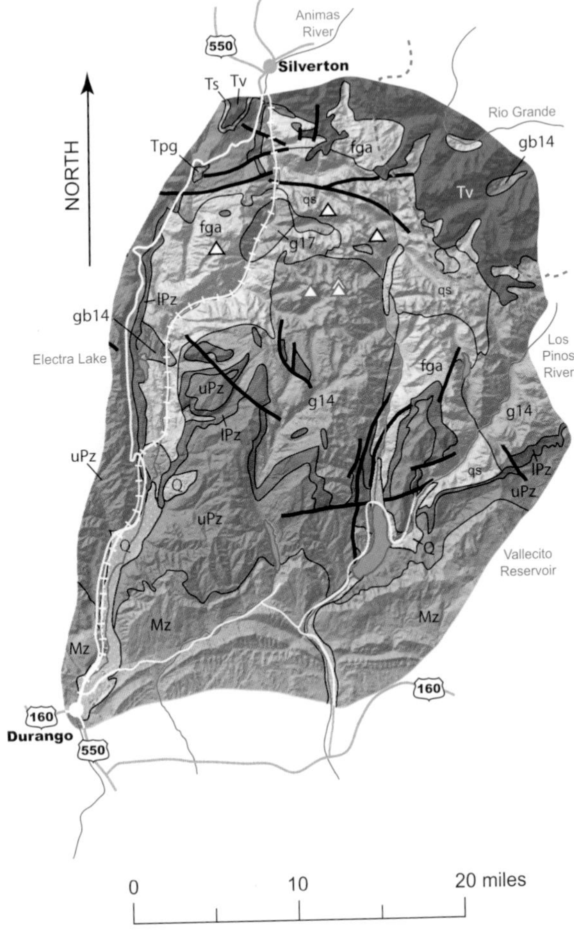

Geologic map of the Needle Mountains.

EXPLANATION

Quaternary deposits
(deposited by streams, glaciers, landslides, or other surficial processes)

Tertiary volcanic rocks

Tertiary porphyry and granite (intruded after the Laramide orogeny)

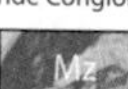

Tertiary sedimentary rocks (Telluride Conglomerate)

Mesozoic sedimentary rocks (mostly deposited in or near the great Cretaceous seaway)

Upper Paleozoic sedimentary rocks (mostly deposited during uplift and erosion of the Ancestral Rocky Mountains)

lPz

Lower Paleozoic sedimentary rocks (deposited in shallow seas)

Basement Rocks

Plutonic rocks intruded about 1.4 billion years ago

Granite

Gabbro

Quartzite, schist and related rocks (Uncompahgre Formation)

Felsic gneiss and amphibolite

Symbols

Geologic contact

High-angle fault

Explanation for geologic map of the Needle Mountains.

A very diverse array of Precambrian basement rocks crop out in the core of the Needle Mountain uplift. Metamorphic rocks predominate in the western part of the range, massive granite makes up the central part, and tightly folded and faulted but less metamorphosed sedimentary rocks lie in a northwest-trending belt in the northeastern part.

The metamorphic rocks in the western part of the range are exposed in the West Needle Mountains around Twilight Peak and in much of the canyon of the Animas River. They are chiefly layered gneiss, amphibolite, schist, and granite gneiss. The layered gneiss and schist were probably formed by metamorphism of ancient volcanic and sedimentary rocks; the granite gneiss probably formed by metamorphism and shearing of a body of granitic rock that intruded the layered rocks before they were metamorphosed. The metamorphic rocks have been dated between 1.8 and 1.75 billion years old (roughly the same age as similar rocks in many other parts of Colorado). The topography sculpted in them is reminiscent of that of the Front Range and the Park Range. East of Vallecito Creek in the eastern part of the range the layered gneisses are less deformed and metamorphosed and display features that attest to their sedimentary and volcanic origins, including pillow-shaped masses formed when lava flows spilled into water, volcanic breccia, and sedimentary bedding formed as finer volcanic debris was deposited in water.

The sedimentary rocks in the northeastern part of the range are chiefly quartzite, conglomerate, slate, and schist that were deposited after the older rocks had been metamorphosed, deformed, and intruded by bodies of granite dated as about 1.7 billion years old. The sedimentary rocks (called the Uncompahgre Formation) were squeezed into tight accordion-like northwest-trending folds that define the outcrop belt of the formation. Because of the tough resistant nature of the quartzite and conglomerates, they were shaped by erosion into the jagged aligned peaks of the Grenadier Range with fascinating names including Arrow, Vestal, Trinity, Storm King, and The Guardian. Although the range contains no Fourteeners, according to *Guide to the Colorado Mountains:*

> *"The Grenadiers offer some of the finest mountaineering in the entire state. Soaring faces of white quartzite, remote alpine campsites, and pristine wilderness, have gladdened the hearts of Colorado climbers since the days of pitons and hob-nailed boots. . . . If you travel in this country, bring a rope and friends you trust."*

Although small bodies of quartzite and related rocks have been mapped in the Park Range, Front Range, and Sawatch Range, nowhere else in Colorado do they form challenging peaks comparable to those of the Grenadier Range. The canyon of Vallecito Creek and the lower part of the canyon of the Los Pinos River in the southeastern part of the range have been carved in separate bodies of quartzite and conglomerate that are probably equivalent to the Uncompahgre Formation, but these bodies form no major peaks.

The Eolus Granite, the large body of granite that forms the central parts of the Needle Mountains, was emplaced about 1.435 billion years ago, after deposition and folding of the Uncompahgre Formation. It is a coarse-grained, gray to pink granite, commonly containing large, rectangular, pink feldspar crystals that weather out to form convenient fingerholds and toeholds for the technical climber. It tends to weather into large, irregular blocks like those that form the much-photographed summit of Sunlight Peak and its neighboring Fourteeners, Mt. Eolus and Windom Peak. The peaks in this part of the range are just as rugged and nearly as spectacular as those in the Grenadier Range, but because the granite is massive and lacks any conspicuous streaky

Sunlight Peak from the summit of Windom Peak. The jagged ridge joining the peaks is closely jointed pink granite of the Eolus batholith. The streak of reddish rock in the saddle south of Sunlight probably marks a minor fault. The prominent peak in the middle distance near the right edge of the picture is Arrow Peak in the Grenadier Range. VAN WILLIAMS PHOTO

Steeply north-sloping layers of quartzite in the Uncompahgre Formation form the Trinity Peaks in the Grenadier Range.

DAVE GASKILL PHOTO

orientation of minerals, the valleys and ridges tend to be more randomly oriented than those carved in the quartzite layers of the Uncompahgre Formation.

Although of little interest to climbers, the small body of gabbro along the Animas Canyon is fascinating to geologists because it is one of the few examples of gabbro emplaced at about the same time as the 1.4-billion-year-old granitic rocks that are so widespread in the Colorado mountains.

San Miguel Mountains

The San Miguel Mountains are a spur of the main San Juan mountain complex that projects from near Lizard Head Pass for about twenty miles westward toward the Colorado Plateau. The San Miguels are a relatively small but extremely rugged range that includes three Fourteeners, Wilson Peak, Mt. Wilson, and El Diente, as well as the spectacular spire of Lizard Head. Although they are geographically part of the San Juans, their geology and therefore their topographic character are completely different from either the main volcanic parts of the San Juans or the basement rocks of the Needle Mountains.

In many ways the geology of the San Miguels is more similar to that of the West Elk Mountains than it is to the other parts of the San Juans. The range is largely made up of Cretaceous rocks, chiefly flat-lying shale and sandstone deposited in the Cretaceous Seaway, intruded by a complex array of sills, dikes, and irregular stocks of igneous rocks that form many of the highest peaks and ridges, including Wilson Peak and El Diente. Mt. Wilson is capped by an erosional remnant of volcanic breccia intruded and altered by myriad dikes of porphyry and granite. The treacherous ridge between Mt. Wilson and El Diente, which is noted among climbers for its highly unstable rock, lies partly in granite and partly in altered volcanic breccia cut by similar dikes. The imposing 300-foot-high spire of Lizard Head is also composed of volcanic rocks. The base of the spire is dark volcanic breccia, most of the spire is made up of thin flows of dark lava, and the summit is capped by volcanic breccia like that at the base. The occurrence of these scraps of volcanic rocks suggests that the San Juan volcanic field originally extended west over much or all of the San Miguel Range.

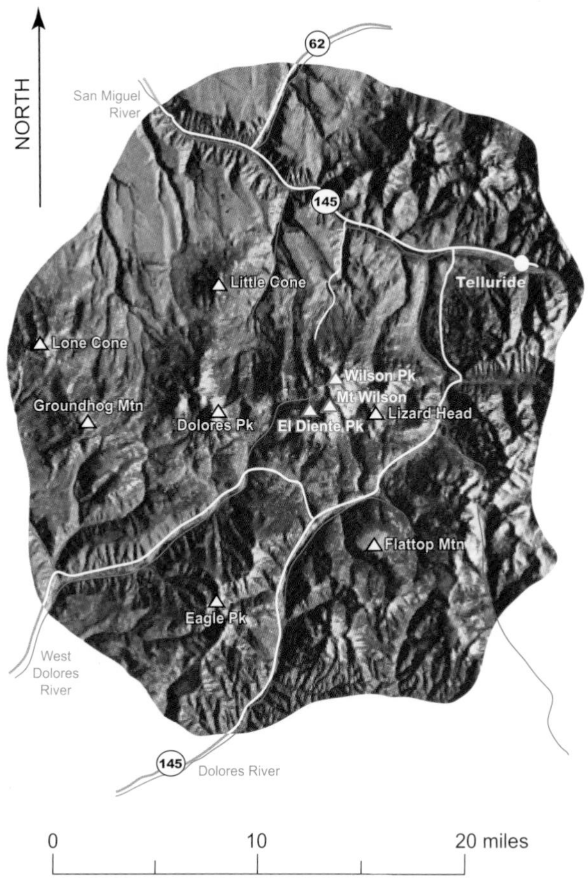

Satellite image of the San Miguel Mountains showing geographic features.

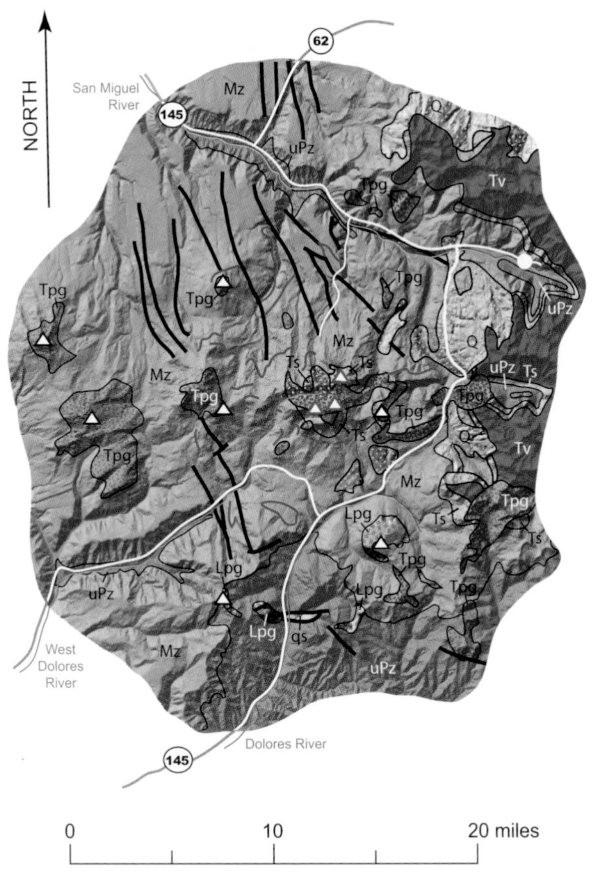

Geologic map of the San Miguel Mountains.

EXPLANATION

Quaternary deposits
(deposited by streams, glaciers, landslides,
or other surficial processes)

Tertiary volcanic rocks

Tertiary porphyry and granite
(intruded after the
Laramide orogeny)

Tertiary sedimentary rocks
(Telluride Conglomerate)

Porphyry and granite
(intruded during the Laramide orogeny)

Mesozoic sedimentary rocks
(mostly deposited in or near the great
Cretaceous seaway)

Upper Paleozoic sedimentary rocks
(mostly deposited during uplift and erosion
of the Ancestral Rocky Mountains)

Basement Rocks

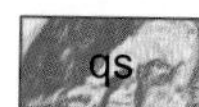

Quartzite, schist and
related rocks
(Uncompahgre Formation)

Symbols

Geologic contact

High-angle fault

Dikes and sills

Explanation for geologic map of the San Miguel Mountains.

The intrusive igneous rocks are light- to medium-gray and generally fine-grained granite and porphyry. Some contain conspicuous lath-shaped crystals of white or pink feldspar half an inch or less in length that formed early in the crystallization of the magma. Some of the igneous bodies are flat-floored pillow-shaped bodies called laccoliths. Some form sills (sheets parallel to the layers in the enclosing sedimentary rocks). The sills are a few feet to as much as 1,500 feet thick, and at least one can be traced along the mountainsides for almost ten miles. The largest igneous bodies are irregular stocks. The largest of these stocks is the Mt. Wilson stock, which is exposed in Navajo Basin between Mt. Wilson and Wilson Peak. It crops out in an east-west-trending belt at least five miles long and as much as two miles

The treacherous Wilson-El Diente ridge as seen from the summit of Mount Wilson. The dark area in the center of the picture is a cloud shadow placed by fate to frustrate the photographer. VAN WILLIAMS PHOTO

wide. It was probably emplaced at depths of a mile or less beneath the land surface, but whether or not it fed volcanic eruptions at the surface is not clear. The stock is surrounded by a zone as much as two miles wide in which the enclosing Cretaceous shale has been heated, bleached, and metamorphosed to slate and hornfels, making it extremely resistant to

Lizard Head. The spire itself is volcanic breccia and lava flows; the slopes below are Cretaceous shale laced with dikes and sills of white porphyry. Outcrop in the foreground is a thin sill of porphyry sandwiched in black shale; the diagonal wall on the slopes below the peak is a dike of porphyry. STEVE HOFFMEYER PHOTO

erosion. It makes up many of the ridges flanking the high peaks.

Precise dates on the igneous rocks are not yet available. The Mt. Wilson stock cuts some of the caldera-fed ash flows, so it must be younger than 30 million years. The nearby Ophir stock has been dated at about 26 million years, and the igneous rocks in the San Miguels are probably of about the same age. Thus, they may give us a view of the igneous bodies that form the roots of the calderas elsewhere in the San Juans.

The present topography of the San Miguels was carved during the last period of erosion of the San Juan volcanic plateau, mostly during the last 5 million years. Although the San Miguel Range was too small to support an ice cap like other parts of the San Juans, it hosted several large valley glaciers. One of these extended from Navajo Basin at least seven miles to the vicinity of Dunton; another headed in the basin between Mt. Wilson and Gladstone Peak and extended almost five miles—nearly to the Dolores River; and a third headed in Silver Pick Basin and advanced northward all the way to the San Miguel River. During and after the last glaciation, extensive landslides formed on the unstable Cretaceous shale on the lower slopes of the range, and after the ice retreat the basins and cirques were festooned with talus and rock glaciers.

FIVE

The Riddle of the Fourteeners

Why Are There No Fifteeners?

Although many mountains in other parts of North America are far higher than those in Colorado, the state has the distinction of having the highest average elevation of any state in the Union. It also contains the largest area with average elevation above 10,000 feet anywhere in North America. Although many other North American ranges stand higher above their surrounding lowlands and pose greater mountaineering challenges, the Colorado mountains are unique in several ways. They include more than half the named peaks with elevations over 14,000 feet on the continent. They lie farther from the western edge of the North American tectonic plate than any other major group of mountains—750 to 900 miles, while all other high ranges are less than 350 miles—and most are less than 250 miles—from the plate margin. And finally, while there are fifty-four or more Fourteeners (depending on whose guidebook you read), all of their summit elevations lie within a narrow range between 14,001-foot Sunshine Peak and 14,433-foot Mt. Elbert. This last is perhaps the greatest riddle of all. Why should so many peaks with such diverse rocks and varied geologic histories in a dozen different ranges spread over an area two hundred miles long and less than a hundred miles wide all have summit elevations within a few hundred feet of one another? Why are there no "Fifteeners" in Colorado? Why are there no Fourteeners in any of the adjoining states?

The answers to these questions must lie in the behavior of the Earth's crust and the deeper Earth layers that lie below it. On the continents the crust generally has a composition approximately like that of granite and is generally about twenty-five miles thick. The mantle, which lies below the crust, consists of material that is much lower in silica, sodium, and potassium, and richer in magnesium and iron. The crust and the upper part of the mantle are relatively rigid and together make up the lithosphere. The lower part of the mantle where the material is plastic and flows readily is called the asthenosphere. It is the interactions between the crust and mantle and between the lithosphere and the asthenosphere that give birth to mountains.

How High are the Fourteeners?

The official elevations of many of Colorado's Fourteeners have recently gone up between five and seven feet! Sometime in the indefinite future when new maps come out, you will see some new numbers. For example, the elevation of Mt. Elbert will become 14,440 feet; Pikes Peak will become 14,115 feet; Torreys will become 14,275 feet; and Snowmass will be 14,099 feet.

As we have seen earlier, the peaks still may be going up, but probably at rates of fractions of a millimeter per year, so slow that it would be scarcely noticeable in several lifetimes! If so, why have the elevations suddenly increased by several feet? The answer is that the National Geodetic Survey—the federal agency responsible for determining the precise locations and elevations of survey points throughout the U.S., including those brass tablets you find on many summits—has readjusted the network of carefully surveyed level lines that crisscross the country.

When a surveyor measures elevations in the field, the measurement is from an imaginary surface called the geoid. The geoid is a surface that is everywhere perpendicular to a plumb line (the direction of a string with a weight suspended from it, like a surveyor's plumb bob) and that most closely approximates the average surface of the oceans. If you could place a frictionless marble on the geoid (it would have to be an imaginary marble, since the geoid is an imaginary surface) the marble would not roll in any direction. The geoid is somewhat irregular. In flat areas, it is relatively smooth, but near mountains it is deflected upward because the extra mass of the mountains attracts a plumb bob. Even at the ocean surface the geoid is slightly irregular because of the dynamic of ocean currents and the gravitational attraction of undersea mountains.

The elevations shown on all current U.S. Geological Survey maps are measured with respect to the National Geodetic Vertical Datum of 1929 (NGVD 29), which is based on a geoid calculated before modern data on regional gravity variations were available. The new elevations are calculated with respect to the North American Vertical Datum of 1988 (NAVD 88), which is based on a new geoid calculated from modern gravity information and hundreds of new survey lines.

The maximum shifts in elevations are in the western United States, particularly in the high mountains of Colorado and Wyoming, where gravity variations are greatest. In the central parts of the country changes are minimal. The changes in elevation are not enough to produce any new Fourteeners, although Grizzly Peak (the one south of Independence Pass) will miss by only five or six feet instead of twelve feet. Nor do they change the elevation you need to gain to reach the summit—the trailheads and everything else goes up the same amount. In this book, we stick with the NGVD 29 elevations in order to be consistent with available topographic maps.

The crust beneath the Colorado mountains ranges in thickness from about twenty-seven to more than thirty-four miles, about the same as that beneath the plains to the east, but somewhat thicker than average continental crust. However, in many places the upper mantle beneath the mountains is warmer and more plastic than that beneath the plains.

We know from deep drilling that metamorphic rocks and granites similar to those that make up the basement in many of the Colorado ranges extend eastward beneath flat-lying younger sedimentary rocks of the plains for hundreds of miles. Basement-cored uplifts related to the Paleozoic Ancestral Rocky Mountains also lie covered by the same sedimentary blanket. Thus, neither uplift related to formation of the basement rocks nor that related to the rise of the Ancestral Rocky Mountains can have played a direct role in the elevation of the present peaks, even though many of them are carved in basement rocks or in redbeds related to the Ancestral Rockies.

All of Colorado's high mountains lie within the region affected by the Laramide orogeny, during which the crust was shortened and thickened by east-west or northeast-southwest compression. However, the Laramide orogeny also affected the crust in parts of Montana, much of western Wyoming, and New Mexico. While these areas all have spectacular, high mountains, none has a 14,000-foot peak. This suggests that the Laramide orogeny is not the sole cause of Colorado's Fourteeners. Other evidence supports this conclusion.

As we have seen, the highlands raised during the Laramide orogeny were largely leveled by subsequent erosion, producing a landscape of low hills and broad valleys, but perhaps including a few mountains cored by erosion resistant rocks. Remnants of this old, post-Laramide landscape are preserved as the flat-topped ridges and rolling uplands in many parts of south-central Colorado ranges, including parts of the Front Range, Mosquito Range, Sawatch Range and South Park. This surface developed gradually during and after the waning stages of the Laramide orogeny, beginning perhaps as early as 50 million years ago. The same surface lies buried beneath 33-to-35-million-year-old volcanic rocks in the northern and southern Front Range, the northern Gore Range, the Sawatch Range, and especially in the San Juan Mountains, where the Telluride Conglomerate was deposited in valleys on the surface before it was buried by the pre-caldera volcanic rocks.

All of the San Juan Fourteeners are formed of rocks that are younger than the post-Laramide land surface. These include Mt. Sneffels and Wetterhorn Peak, both carved from plugs of intrusive igneous rocks intruded about 25 or 26 million years ago; Handies Peak and Uncompahgre Peak, carved in dark lava, breccia, and conglomerate; and Redcloud, Sunlight, and San Luis Peaks, carved in ash-flow tuffs, some as young as 23 million years. In the Sawatch Range, Mt. Princeton, Mt. Antero, Tabeguache Mountain, and Mt. Shavano are all carved from granite in the 34-million-year-old Mt. Princeton batholith and thus must have been carved by erosion during uplift much later than the Laramide uplift.

What caused this late episode of uplift? One theory is that the upper mantle beneath the Colorado mountains was heated and charged with water and other volatile components during subduction related to the Laramide orogeny. Pre-existing zones of

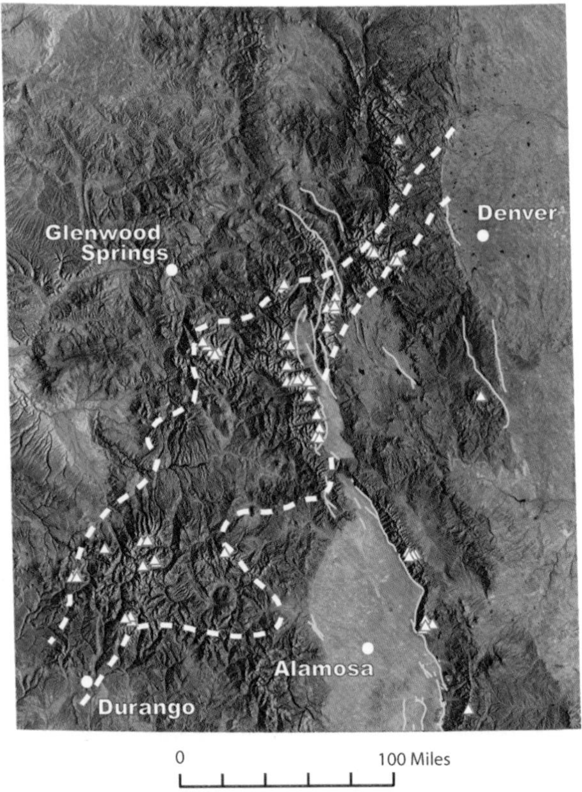

Distribution of the Colorado Fourteeners (red and white triangles) in relation to the Colorado Mineral Belt (white dotted lines) and the Rio Grande Rift (pale yellow with related young faults shown by yellow lines).

weakness in the crust served as conduits for heat and for the rise of magmas that fed intrusions both during the Laramide and during the post-Laramide volcanic flare-up. Both the injection of the magma bodies (some of which erupted as calderas) and warming of the surrounding rocks (which would cause them to rise because the rocks expand and become less dense) would lead to uplift of the land surface. One such zone of warm viscous upper mantle lies approximately along the Colorado Mineral Belt. Another zone of weakness was the Rio Grande rift, which began opening about 32 million years ago in southern New Mexico. Gradually the tip of the opening rift worked its way northward, reaching into Colorado about 26 million years ago. As the rift opened, its flanks tended to rise, partly because of outflow of material at depth beneath the subsiding rift floor and partly because of warming of the flanking rocks.

All but two of the Fourteeners (Pikes Peak and Longs Peak) lie on one or the other flank of the Rio Grande Rift or in the Colorado Mineral Belt, and the highest and most numerous are near Leadville, where the rift and the mineral belt intersect. Notice that the number and heights of the Fourteeners on the rift flanks decreases southward. This is because the uplift of the flanks of the rift is greater near the active tip of the rift, and decreases in the earlier opened parts of the rift farther to the south—one reason why there are no Fourteeners in New Mexico. It appears that Colorado may owe its surprising number of Fourteeners to a lucky coincidence: the Laramide orogeny, the Colorado Mineral Belt, and the active tip of the Rio Grande rift. The relatively accordant height to the highest peaks must be the result of more or less uniform uplift of a fairly flat land surface (part of which is preserved as the flat post-volcanic plateau surface in the San Juans) and concurrent erosion that left the most favorably located and most resistant rocks standing at more or less the same level.

SIX

The End, But Also the Beginning of the Story

"Mountains are the bones of the Earth, the highest peaks are invariably those parts of its anatomy which in the plains lie buried under five and twenty thousand feet of solid thickness of superincumbent soil, and which spring up in the mountain ranges in vast pyramids or wedges, flinging their garment of earth away from them on each side. The masses of the lower hills are laid over and against their sides, like the masses of lateral masonry against the skeleton arch of an unfinished bridge, except that they slope up and lean against the central ridge; and finally, upon the slopes of these lower hills are strewed the level beds of sprinkled gravel, sand, and clay; which form the extent of the champaign. Here then is another grand principle of the truth of earth, that the mountains must come from under all, and be the support of all; and that everything else must be laid in their arms, heap after heap, the plains being uppermost."

JOHN RUSKIN
from "*The Truth of Earth*"

We come to the end of the story as we've told it, but not to the end of the Real Story: the long and fascinating history of our beloved Colorado mountains, writ in stone for all to see, if only observers would spend a little time and a little intellectual energy to do so.

We've given you some tools and some hints on how to use them. We've laid out the basic framework of the geologic history and the general structure of the rocks that make up the varied ranges in Colorado. We hope that in some small measure we've been able to interest you in pursuing the study of these rocks, a study that can be at times enjoyable and at other times just plain bewildering. If you desire additional information about any of the subjects discussed in these pages, we encourage you to delve into the references listed on page 227, or, even better, search out more details on the Internet or at your local library.

You need only to keep your eyes and mind open as you stride across the alpine tundra or trudge up the slopes. Don't hesitate to explore the geology of our beautiful mountains. If our own experiences are any guide, we can assure you that, even though you might never receive answers to all of your many questions, you'll be the better for asking them. And who knows, maybe you will be the one who sees it all clearly in the end and can then enlighten the rest of us.

APPENDIX

EXHIBIT 2
Geology of the Fourteeners

Elevations (in feet) are from U.S. Geological Survey 7½ minute quadrangles and are based on the National Geodetic Vertical Datum of 1929. Peaks are listed from north to south in each range except as noted

FRONT RANGE

NAME: **Longs Peak**

ELEVATION: 14,255

ROCKS: Mountain largely composed of light-gray granite of the Longs Peak–St. Vrain batholith emplaced about 1.4 billion years ago. Parts of the north and west flanks of the peak are biotite schist and migmatite in irregular slabs that were included in the magma as the granite was injected. During magma flowage, tabular domino-sized crystals of potassium feldspar were aligned in sub-horizontal planes, giving the granite a streaky appearance.

REMARKS: The famous East Face is formed by near-vertical joints in granite at the head of a cirque carved by the glacier that flowed down the Roaring Fork of Cabin Creek, depositing the Mills moraine.

NAME: **Grays Peak** **ELEVATION:** 14,270

NAME: **Torreys Peak** **ELEVATION:** 14,267

ROCKS: Both peaks largely interlayered gray biotite gneiss, schist, and migmatite, cut by dikes of pegmatite. Southwest slopes near summit of Torreys Peak are granite and porphyry related to the 35-million-year-old Montezuma stock, which underlies much of the upper basin of Peru Creek. Dikes of porphyry cut the gneiss and schist on the Kelso Ridge (northeast ridge) of Torreys Peak. Small northeast-trending faults cut the gneiss and schist between the peaks and on the north face of Torreys Peak.

REMARKS: These are the only Colorado Fourteeners that are on the Continental Divide. Grays Peak has the distinction of being the highest point on the Continental Divide in North America.

NAME: **Mount Evans** **ELEVATION:** 14,264
NAME: **Mount Bierstadt** **ELEVATION:** 14,065

ROCKS: Both peaks are in granite of the 1.4-billion-year-old Mount Evans batholith. The granite is somewhat darker colored than most granites of the same age in the Front Range and contains thin wispy accumulations of biotite and other dark minerals that give the rock a streaky appearance. The streaks are generally flattened in planes that trend roughly east-west and are inclined moderately to steeply toward the north. The rock contains so much magnetite (magnetic iron oxide) that in places it affects a compass.

REMARKS: The flanks of these peaks are scalloped by deep cirques. The Sawtooth northeast of Mt. Bierstadt is the narrow jagged ridge between two cirques, as is the summit ridge of Mt. Evans. However, broad smooth areas on the surrounding ridges have not been glaciated.

NAME: **Pikes Peak**
ELEVATION: 14,110

ROCKS: Mountain made up largely of coarse-grained pink to pale orange homogeneous granite of the 1.0-billion-year-old Pikes Peak batholith; irregular bodies of slightly younger pink fine-grained granite with scattered large feldspar crystals cut the main granite near the summit. Rocks are cut by two sets of near-vertical joints one of which trends north-northeast and the other east-northeast.

REMARKS: Peak lies near the center of an elliptical area surrounded by faults within which the rocks have been uplifted relative to surrounding parts of the batholith. This may represent the roots of an old caldera where the batholith vented to the surface.

TENMILE AND MOSQUITO RANGES

NAME: **Quandary Peak**
ELEVATION: 14,265

ROCKS: Most of the mountain is basement rock, chiefly biotite gneiss and migmatite with many dikes of pegmatite. Summit and lower part of east ridge are capped by east-sloping layers of lower Paleozoic sedimentary rocks, chiefly sandstone, shale, and limestone.

All rocks are cut by dikes of post-Laramide granite and porphyry.

REMARKS: One porphyry dike about 150 feet thick cuts through the east ridge just east of the summit.

NAME: Mount Lincoln **ELEVATION:** 14,286

NAME: Mount Bross **ELEVATION:** 14,172

ROCKS: Lower slopes are basement rocks, chiefly biotite gneiss, migmatite, and granite. High ridge connecting the peaks is capped by 500 feet or more of flat-lying lower Paleozoic sandstone, shale, and limestone, broken by a complicated array of faults. Summit of both peaks is capped by post-Laramide porphyry which forms a sill intruded into the sedimentary rocks.

REMARKS: Entire area around the peaks has been extensively prospected and mined, chiefly for silver. Sweet Home mine southeast of Mt. Bross is source of museum-quality crystals of rhodochrosite (manganese carbonate), Colorado's state mineral.

NAME: Mount Democrat

ELEVATION: 14,148

ROCKS: Mountain is entirely in basement rocks. Summit and east ridges are in coarse-grained streaky granite, probably emplaced about 1.7 billion years ago. Northern slopes are in light-colored granite of the 1.4-billion-year age group. Western slopes are chiefly biotite gneiss and migmatite. All of these rocks are cut by numerous dikes of Laramide porphyry and granite.

REMARKS: The north-south-trending Mosquito fault passes about 2 miles west of the summit. West of the fault Paleozoic sedimentary rocks have dropped down almost 10,000 feet relative to the basement rocks on the summit. This displacement probably took place during opening of the Rio Grande rift.

NAME: Mount Sherman

ELEVATION: 14,036

ROCKS: Entire mountain is in sill of dense fine-grained white porphyry that intruded into Paleozoic sedimentary rocks during the Laramide orogeny. Offset on a fault on the southern slopes of the mountain nearly double the apparent thickness of the sill.

REMARKS: Dreary topography and loose talus and scree combine to make this one of the least attractive of the Fourteeners.

SAWATCH RANGE

NAME: Mount of the Holy Cross

ELEVATION: 14,005

ROCKS: Biotite gneiss, schist, and migmatite. Layering in gneiss and schistosity in schist trend north-south and are steeply inclined, generally to the west. Rocks are cut by northeast-trending dikes of granite and porphyry.

REMARKS: Northeast-southwest-trending fault forms a steep couloir on the northeast face of the mountain in which snow accumulates to form the vertical part of the cross. The horizontal arm is formed by accumulation of snow on ledges marking west-sloping joints at right angles to the fault.

NAME: Mount Elbert

ELEVATION: 14,433

ROCKS: Biotite gneiss, schist, and migmatite. Layering in gneiss and schistosity in schist trend northwest-southeast and are steeply inclined or vertical. Cut by dikes of white porphyry and granite dated at about 38 million years. Lower southern and southeastern slopes are dark-gray-brown streaky 1.7-billion-year-old granite.

REMARKS: Highest peak in Colorado. Extensive glacial deposits mantle eastern slopes to elevations up to 12,000 feet.

NAME: Mount Massive

ELEVATION: 14,421

ROCKS: Summit is 1.4-billion-year-old granite. High ridges to north and south are biotite gneiss, schist, and migmatite.

NAME: La Plata Peak

ELEVATION: 14,336

ROCKS: Summit is dark grayish brown streaky 1.7-billion-year-old granite. Lower slopes are light-gray granite of the 65-million-year-old Twin Lakes batholith. Older granite is cut by several dikes of light-colored porphyry

REMARKS: Granite at the summit is part of the original roof of the Twin Lakes batholith.

NAME: Huron Peak
ELEVATION: 14,003
ROCKS: Most of the mountain is made up of light-gray to tan medium- to coarse-grained 65-million-year-old granite of the Twin Lakes batholith. On the southwest slopes the granite passes into a darker colored hornblende rich igneous rock intermediate between granite and gabbro. Summit and upper ridges are light-gray rudely layered granite that is part of the basement.
REMARKS: Basement granite that forms summit of Huron has been dated as about 1.65 billion years old, significantly younger than the basement granite on Mount Belford.

NAME: Mount Belford **ELEVATION:** 14,197
NAME: Mount Oxford **ELEVATION:** 14,153
NAME: Missouri Mountain **ELEVATION:** 14,069
ROCKS: All three peaks are in dark coarse-grained 1.7-billion-year-old granite like that on Harvard and Columbia. Streaky structure trends north-south and slopes west on Oxford and Belford and east on Missouri.
REMARKS: Around Elkhead Pass between Belford and Missouri part of the ridge is formed by light-tan porphyry related to the Twin Lakes batholith.

NAME: Mount Harvard **ELEVATION:** 14,420
NAME: Mount Columbia **ELEVATION:** 14,073
ROCKS: Both peaks are in coarse-grained dark biotite-rich gray 1.7-billion-year-old granite. Granite contains scattered large white feldspar crystals and has a streaky structure formed by crushing and deformation during metamorphism. Streaky structure trends north-south and is generally near vertical.
REMARKS: South ridge of Harvard and west slopes of Columbia are in slightly younger light-gray rudely layered granite that has been dated as about 1.65 billion years old and which escaped the crushing and deformation that affected the older granite.

NAME: **Mount Yale**
ELEVATION: 14,196
ROCKS: Most of mountain is a chaotic mixture of fine- to coarse-grained light-colored granite and fine-grained nearly white plutonic igneous rock. On the summit ridge of Mount Yale the granites contain several narrow irregular bodies of dark greenish gabbro. Streaky structure in the granite trends generally east-west and slopes south.
REMARKS: The granites and gabbro are all part of the basement, and pre-date the coarse-grained granite that makes up Mounts Harvard and Columbia.

NAME: **Mount Princeton** **ELEVATION:** 14,197
NAME: **Mount Antero** **ELEVATION:** 14,269
ROCKS: Both mountains are in the Mount Princeton batholith, a large body of uniform light-gray medium-grained granite emplaced about 34.3 million years ago, slightly before formation of the Mount Aetna caldera. Although the summit of Mount Antero lies in granite typical of the batholith, the southern slopes are in slightly younger and lighter colored granite. It is this granite that hosts the pegmatite dikes and open cavities that contain the crystals of aquamarine and other rare minerals for which the mountain is famous.
REMARKS: The Chalk Cliffs along Chalk Creek south of Mount Princeton are not chalk at all—they are granite of the Mount Princeton batholith in which the rock has been largely altered to white clay by water from hot springs.

NAME: **Tabeguache Mountain**
ELEVATION: 14,155
ROCKS: Peak lies just west of the edge of the Mount Princeton batholith in a narrow wedge of 1.7-billion-year-old streaky granite; southeastern slopes and nearby parts of east ridge are in a large dike of light-colored granite that contains large rectangular white and pink feldspar crystals and large round grains of gray quartz.
REMARKS: The dike, which is related to the Mount Princeton granite, lies along the contact between the batholith and the 1.7-billion-year-old basement granite.

NAME: **Mount Shavano**

ELEVATION: 14,229

ROCKS: Summit and northwest ridge are in granite of the Mount Princeton batholith. Eastern slopes are in basement rocks, chiefly 1.7-billion-year-old granite and interlayered gneiss and amphibolite.

REMARKS: The famous snow angel of Shavano is formed by accumulation of snow in intersecting gullies in the basin southeast of the summit. The angel's head marks the contact between the batholith and the basement rocks.

SANGRE DE CRISTO MOUNTAINS

NAME: **Kit Carson Mountain**

ELEVATION: 14,165

ROCKS: Entire peak is composed of red conglomerate with some beds of red sandstone and minor beds of red shale. Pebbles, cobbles, and boulders in the conglomerate commonly weather out to form secure handholds and footholds. Bedding trends northwest and is inclined toward the northeast at angles of about 45°; jagged summit ridge is broken by near-vertical northeast-trending joints which form steep couloirs. Northeast slopes are smooth and parallel to bedding; southwest slopes are steep stair steps across bedding.

REMARKS: Challenger Point (14,060) about 0.2 miles west of summit is included as a separate peak on some lists of Fourteeners.

NAME: **Humboldt Peak**

ELEVATION: 14,064

ROCKS: Peak is chiefly red sandstone with some beds of conglomerate and a few beds of red shale. Beds trend generally east-west and are gently inclined to the south, so south slopes are smooth and featureless and north slopes are cliffy.

NAME: **Crestone Peak** **ELEVATION:** 14,294

NAME: **Crestone Needle** **ELEVATION:** 14,197

ROCKS: Both peaks are in red conglomerate with a few sandstone beds. Some boulders in conglomerate are the size of Volkswagens. Beds trend northwest and are steeply inclined to the southwest, so northeast faces of the peaks are very steep but relatively secure while southwest faces are somewhat less jagged, but more subject to rockfall. Steep northeast-trending joints form couloirs that notch the jagged ridge between the Peak and the Needle.

NAME: Ellingwood Point
ELEVATION: 14,042
ROCKS: Peak is composed of dark greenish gabbro with small crystals of green hornblende and white plagioclase imbedded in a finer grained gray material. Rocks on summit ridge broken by several faults. Crest of the northeast ridge is a dike of light-colored post-Laramide porphyry.

NAME: Mount Lindsey
ELEVATION: 14,042
ROCKS: Summit and upper ridges composed of tonolite, a very light colored fine-grained intrusive igneous rock composed chiefly of plagioclase feldspar and quartz. Tonolite is cut by numerous northwest-trending dikes of gabbro and basalt. One of these dikes about 150 feet wide crosses north face just below the summit. Lower slopes are chiefly amphibolite.
REMARKS: A thin slice of upper Paleozoic gray sandstone and shale between two thrust faults crosses the ridge between Mount Lindsey and the Iron Nipple.

NAME: Blanca Peak **ELEVATION:** 14,345
NAME: Little Bear Peak **ELEVATION:** 14,037
ROCKS: Both peaks and the sawtooth ridge between them are composed of dark greenish gabbro like that on Ellingwood Point. In many places angular blocks of the dark rock several feet in diameter are surrounded by lighter colored igneous rock like the tonolite on Mount Lindsey. Ridge between the summits is broken by several faults and cut by dikes of post-Laramide granite and porphyry, making it very unstable.
One guidebook remarks that the ridge between the peaks "... is rickety and gives us the impression that it must be held together."

NAME: **Culebra Peak**

ELEVATION: 14,047

ROCKS: Mountain is in a complex block of basement rocks that has been carried eastward on west-sloping thrust faults across upper Paleozoic and Mesozoic rocks. Uppermost of these thrust faults lies about 2 miles east of summit. Summit and upper slopes are in dark, rudely layered biotite and hornblende gneiss cut by dikes of pegmatite; southeast slopes are in interlayered felsic gneiss and amphibolite. Layering and streaky structure in gneiss trends roughly east-west and is inclined gently to moderately north. Lower parts of western slopes are coarse-grained streak 1.7-billion-year-old granite.

REMARKS: Culebra misses by nine miles being the highest peak in New Mexico instead of the 41st highest in Colorado.

ELK MOUNTAINS

NAME: **Capitol Peak**

ELEVATION: 14,130

ROCKS: Entire mountain is in irregularly jointed uniform light- to medium-gray medium-grained granite of the Snowmass stock, an irregular body of igneous rock that was intruded into upper Paleozoic redbeds about 34 million years ago. The magma that formed the stock intruded along the Elk Range thrust fault, which carried the Paleozoic rocks southwestward over younger rocks during the Laramide orogeny.

REMARKS: The famous Knife Edge on Capitol is formed by the intersection of two sets of joints in the granite that forms the crest of the jagged northeast ridge between the Pierre Lakes cirque and the Capitol Lake cirque.

NAME: **Snowmass Mountain**

ELEVATION: 14,092

ROCKS: Entire mountain is in granite of the Snowmass stock. Southeast contact of the stock lies southeast of Snowmass Peak and is clearly visible from campsites at the north end of Snowmass Lake. The granite is in contact with brownish gray sandstone and shale originally deposited in the Central Colorado trough. Near the contact the sedimentary rocks are bleached and partly altered to hornfels.

REMARKS: The snow mass from which the mountain takes its name lies on flat slabs of glacially polished granite just east of the summit. It is sometimes visible from peaks in the Front Range more than 75 miles away. In some summers it disappears entirely.

NAME: North Maroon Peak **ELEVATION:** 14,014
NAME: Maroon Peak **ELEVATION:** 14,156
(commonly called South Maroon Peak)

ROCKS: Both peaks are made up of maroon to brick red colored sandstone, shale, and conglomerate and minor limestone of the Maroon Formation, which consists of material deposited during the rise and destruction of the Ancestral Rocky Mountains. Some of the shale beds contain fossil mud cracks, raindrop imprints, and plant fragments. The coarser sandstone and conglomerate beds generally stand out as continuous cliff bands, while the shale and finer sandstone layers form talus-covered benches. Beds in both peaks trend east-west and slope north at angles of 10°–20°. On the lower eastern slopes the rocks are bleached to shades of green and gray by heat and solutions from nearby bodies of granite, some of which crops out on the lower southeast slopes of Maroon Peak. Rocks on both peaks are locally cut by near-vertical dikes of granite and porphyry, many of which trend about east-west.

REMARKS: The alternating layers of resistant rocks (sandstone and conglomerate) and crumbly shale make for unstable slopes, treacherous talus, and difficult route-finding. Lower slopes are guarded by extensive talus slopes and rock glaciers. These peaks are sometimes referred to as "the killer Bells".

NAME: Pyramid Peak
ELEVATION: 14,018

ROCKS: Rocks and difficulties much the same as on the Maroon Peaks. Beds in the sedimentary rocks are nearly horizontal or slope a few degrees northeast. Rocks are locally cut by similar dikes. One sill of dark porphyry is sandwiched between the sedimentary beds a few hundred feet below the summit. Rare fossil amphibian tracks have been found in talus on the north slopes.

REMARKS: One climber we encountered slogging up the talus suggested that this might better be named "Treadmill Peak".

NAME: **Castle Peak**

ELEVATION: 14,265

ROCKS: Peak is composed of nearly flat beds of the Maroon Formation that have been metamorphosed by heat and fluids during emplacement of extensive bodies of 34-million-year-old granite. The characteristic red color has been lost. Sandstone has been converted to gray quartzite, shale to greenish gray hornfels, and limestone to gray or greenish gray marble. The rocks are laced with dikes and sills of white to light-gray granite. Larger bodies of granite crop out on the eastern slopes and on the north ridge.

REMARKS: In some places the metamorphosed sedimentary rocks contain enough magnetite (magnetic iron oxide) to thoroughly confuse a compass. Surrounding cirques are choked with talus and rock glaciers.

NORTHWESTERN VOLCANIC SAN JUAN MOUNTAINS

(peaks are listed from west to east)

NAME: **Mount Sneffels**

ELEVATION: 14,150

ROCKS: Stock of gabbro and dark-gray granitic rocks intruding pre-caldera volcanic breccia, conglomerate, and dark lava. Ash flows cap ridges east and west of peak.

REMARKS: Rocks highly fractured and cut by veins and faults; many slopes unstable.

NAME: **Wetterhorn Peak**

ELEVATION: 14,015

ROCKS: Summit is gray-brown densely welded ash flow tuff; south slopes are dark- to medium-gray pre-caldera lava and breccia.

REMARKS: Tuff was erupted from 28.6-million-year-old Ute Creek caldera.

NAME: **Uncompahgre Peak**
ELEVATION: 14,309
ROCKS: Summit is red-brown lava with layer of sandstone and mud-flow breccia on west slopes. Lower slopes are ash-flow tuff.
REMARKS: North wall of 28.6-million-year-old Uncompahgre caldera passes just north of peak.

NAME: **Handies Peak**
ELEVATION: 14,048
ROCKS: Summit capped by thin gray lava flow and green-gray sandstone; lower slopes are gray to red-brown ash flow tuff and breccia containing huge blocks of pre-caldera lava.
Rocks accumulated during and after collapse of 28.6-million-year-old Uncompahgre caldera.

NAME: **Redcloud Peak**
ELEVATION: 14,034
ROCKS: Hard dark-gray welded tuff, locally much altered and stained, interlayered with landslide breccia. Locally intruded by granite and porphyry.
REMARKS: Tuff fills 23-million-year-old Lake City caldera; breccia formed by collapse of caldera walls. Rocks on Redcloud and Sunshine Peaks are the youngest rocks on any Fourteener.

NAME: **Sunshine Peak**
ELEVATION: 14,001
ROCKS: Hard dark-gray welded tuff; faint streaking slopes gently south.
REMARKS: Tuff fills 23-million-year-old Lake City caldera; caldera wall is about 1 mile south of peak. Rocks on Redcloud and Sunshine Peaks are the youngest rocks on any Fourteener.

NAME: **San Luis Peak**
ELEVATION: 14,014
ROCKS: Most of mountain is dark-gray ash flow tuff intruded by granite and porphyry dikes and sills. Eastern slopes and ridges are dark lava and mud flow breccia.

REMARKS: Tuff fills 26.8-million-year-old Nelson Mountain caldera; dark lava and breccia to east part of volcanic cone built after caldera collapse.

NEEDLE MOUNTAINS

NAME: **Mount Eolus** **ELEVATION:** 14,083
NAME: **Windom Peak** **ELEVATION:** 14,082
NAME: **Sunlight Peak** **ELEVATION:** 14,053

ROCKS: All these peaks are made up of massive gray to pink granite containing rectangular crystals of pink potassium feldspar from ½ to 1½ inches long, which weather out to form useful finger-holds or toe-holds. The granite is cut by sets of steeply inclined joints nearly at right angles, so that it breaks into large rectangular blocks. Stable talus, firm rock, and regular joints make for comfortable scrambling and stable talus.

REMARKS: The granite is part of the Eolus batholith, which occupies much of this part of the Needle Mountains. It has been dated at about 1.4 billion years old.

SAN MIGUEL MOUNTAINS

(peaks listed from west to east)

NAME: **El Diente Peak**

ELEVATION: 14,159

ROCKS: Summit is dark plutonic rock; north slopes are massive gray granite; ridge joining peak with Mt. Wilson is partly granite and partly altered volcanic rocks. Rocks along the ridge are cut by many joints and are very unstable and treacherous.

REMARKS: Peak is along south edge of Mt. Wilson stock, which was probably emplaced about 26 million years ago.

NAME: **Mount Wilson**

ELEVATION: 14,246

ROCKS: North slopes and northeast ridge are granite and porphyry; summit is steeply tilted volcanic breccia and lava flows altered to shades of green, purple, and red by heat from the igneous intrusions.

REMARKS: Peak is along south edge of Mt. Wilson stock, which was probably emplaced about 26 million years ago.

NAME: Wilson Peak

ELEVATION: 14,017

ROCKS: Summit and upper ridges are dark-gray massive plutonic rock; north and east ridges are Telluride Conglomerate and volcanic breccia baked and bleached by igneous intrusion. South and west slopes are fine-grained granite and porphyry.

REMARKS: Peak is along north edge of Mt. Wilson stock, which was probably emplaced about 26 million years ago.

Sources and Additional Reading

Blair, Rob. "Origins of Landscapes" in Blair, Rob, et al. *The Western San Juan Mountains: Their Geology, Ecology, and Human History*. Boulder, Colorado: University of Colorado Press, 1996.

Chronic, Halka and Williams, Felicie. *Roadside Geology of Colorado (2nd ed.)*. Missoula, Montana: Mountain Press, 2002.

Hopkins, Ralph L. and Hopkins, Lindy B. *Hiking Colorado's Geology*. Seattle: The Mountaineers, 2000.

Jacobs, Randy. *Guide to the Colorado Mountains (9th ed.)*. Golden, Colorado: The Colorado Mountain Club Press, 1992.

Mathews, Vincent; Keller-Lynn, K; and Fox, Betty, eds. *Messages in Stone*. Colorado Geological Survey, 2003.

Moore, George E. *Mines, mountain roads, and rocks—geologic road logs of the Ouray area*. Ouray County Historical Society Guidebook Series 1, 2004.

Raup, Omer B. Colorado geologic highway map: Colorado Geological Survey, scale 1:1,000,000. 1991.

Sorrell, Charles A. *Rocks and Minerals—a Guide to Field Identification*. New York: St. Martin's Press, 1973.

Tweto, Ogden, Geologic map of Colorado: U.S. Geological Survey, scale 1:500,000. 1979.

About the Authors

Jack Reed (John C. Reed Jr.) has done geologic mapping for the USGS in various parts of Alaska, the central and southern Appalachians, and the mountains of Wyoming, Colorado, and New Mexico. He has recently completed compilation of the Geologic Map of North America. He retired in 1997, but continues to serve as a Scientist Emeritus. He has climbed most of the Colorado 14ers and is a 50-year member of The Colorado Mountain Club, where he continues to lead trips and teach map reading, GPS, and short courses on various aspects of Colorado geology.

Gene Ellis received degrees in geology from the University of New Hampshire and the University of Colorado. He is the Associate Chief Scientist of the Earth Surface Processes Team of the U.S. Geological Survey in Denver. He has mapped geology, evaluated energy resources, and conducted drilling programs. He has climbed on rock and ice, trudged up endless talus slopes, and suffered his share of adventures and misadventures in the mountains of Colorado.

Index

*Page numbers in **bold** type refer to photographs, illustrations, and maps.*

G

N

Q

R

S